WORLD
HISTORY SERIES ■■■

The French and Indian War

Titles in the World History Series

The French and Indian War

by
Benton and Louise Minks

Lucent Books, P.O. Box 289011, San Diego, CA 92198-9011

Dedication

To Leah and Erin

Acknowledgments

With appreciation to the staff of The Memorial Libraries,
Deerfield, Massachusetts, and Pocumtuck Valley
Memorial Association

Library of Congress Cataloging-in-Publication Data

Minks, Benton.
    The French and Indian war / by Benton Minks and Louise
Minks.
        p. cm.—(World history series)
    Includes bibliographical references and index.
    ISBN 1-56006-236-3 (acid-free)
    1. United States—History—French and Indian Wars, 1755-
1763—Juvenile literature.   [1. United States—History—
French and Indian Wars, 1755-1763.]   I. Minks, Louise. II.
Title.   III. Series.
E199.M65   1995
973.2'6—dc20   93-48833
                                                  CIP
                                                  AC

Contents

FEB   1995

Foreword

Each year on the first day of school, nearly every history teacher faces the task of explaining why his or her students should study history. One logical answer to this question is that exploring what happened in our past explains how the things we often take for granted—our customs, ideas, and institutions—came to be. As statesman and historian Winston Churchill put it, "Every nation or group of nations has its own tale to tell. Knowledge of the trials and struggles is necessary to all who would comprehend the problems, perils, challenges, and opportunities which confront us today." Thus, a study of history puts modern ideas and institutions in perspective. For example, though the founders of the United States were talented and creative thinkers, they clearly did not invent the concept of democracy. Instead, they adapted some democratic ideas that had originated in ancient Greece and with which the Romans, the British, and others had experimented. An exploration of these cultures, then, reveals their very real connection to us through institutions that continue to shape our daily lives.

Another reason often given for studying history is the idea that lessons exist in the past from which contemporary societies can benefit and learn. This idea, although controversial, has always been an intriguing one for historians. Those that agree that society can benefit from the past often quote philosopher George Santayana's famous statement, "Those who cannot remember the past are condemned to repeat it." Historians who ascribe to Santayana's philosophy believe that, for example, studying the events that led up to the major world wars or other significant historical events would allow society to chart a different and more favorable course in the future.

Just as difficult as convincing students to realize the importance of studying history is the search for useful and interesting supplementary materials that present historical events in a context that can be easily understood. The volumes in Lucent Books' World History Series attempt to present a broad, balanced, and penetrating view of the march of history. Ancient Egypt's important wars and rulers, for example, are presented against the rich and colorful backdrop of Egyptian religious, social, and cultural developments. The series engages the reader by enhancing historical events with these cultural contexts. For example, in *Ancient Greece,* the text covers the role of women in that society. Slavery is discussed in *The Roman Empire,* as well as how slaves earned their freedom. The numerous and varied aspects of everyday life in these and other societies are explored in each volume of the series. Additionally, the series covers the major political, cultural, and philosophical ideas as the torch of civilization is passed from ancient Mesopotamia and Egypt, through Greece, Rome, Medieval Europe, and other world cultures, to the modern day.

The material in the series is formatted in a thorough, precise, and organized manner. Each volume offers the reader a comprehensive and clearly written overview of an important historical event or period. The topic under discussion is placed in a broad, historical context. For example, *The Italian Renaissance* begins with a discussion of the High Middle Ages and the loss of central control that allowed certain Italian cities to develop artistically. The book ends by looking forward to the Reformation and interpreting the societal changes that grew out of the Renaissance. Thus, students are not only involved in an historical era, but also enveloped by the events leading up to that era and the events following it.

One important and unique feature in the World History Series is the primary and secondary source quotations that richly supplement each volume. These quotes are useful in a number of ways. First, they allow students access to sources they would not normally be exposed to because of the difficulty and obscurity of the original source. The quotations range from interesting anecdotes to far-sighted cultural perspectives and are drawn from historical witnesses both past and present. Second, the quotes demonstrate how and where historians themselves derive their information on the past as they strive to reach a consensus on historical events. Lastly, all of the quotes are footnoted, familiarizing students with the citation process and allowing them to verify quotes and/or look up the original source if the quote piques their interest.

Finally, the books in the World History Series provide a detailed launching point for further research. Each book contains a bibliography specifically geared toward student research. A second, annotated bibliography introduces students to all the sources the author consulted when compiling the book. A chronology of important dates gives students an overview, at a glance, of the topic covered. Where applicable, a glossary of terms is included.

In short, the series is designed not only to acquaint readers with the basics of history, but also to make them aware that their lives are a part of an ongoing human saga. Perhaps they will then come to the same realization as famed historian Arnold Toynbee. In his monumental work, *A Study of History*, he wrote about becoming aware of history flowing through him in a mighty current, and of his own life "welling like a wave in the flow of this vast tide."

Important Dates in the French and Indian War

1497 1534 1608 1609 1610 1630 1632 1678 1682 1690 1697 1703 1704 1710 1712

1497
John Cabot explores parts of North America.

1534
In the first of three voyages, Jacques Cartier explores the St. Lawrence River to the site of Montreal, for France.

1608
Samuel de Champlain explores the St. Lawrence River region and founds Quebec for France.

1609
Samuel de Champlain explores the area of Lake Champlain, claiming it for France.

1610
Henry Hudson sails up the Hudson River as far as the site of present-day Albany.

1630
Boston is settled by Puritan immigrants from England.

1632
Settlement of Acadia is established by the French.

1678
After a series of battles in New Amsterdam (New York), a treaty between Holland and England transfers all Dutch territory to England.

1682
Robert de La Salle explores the Mississippi River region and claims it all for France.

1690
William Phips leads English colonial attack on Port Royal, Acadia. Phips attempts to take Quebec but fails.

1697
King William's War ends with the Treaty of Ryswick. Acadia is returned to France.

1703
Queen Anne's War between France and England begins in North America.

1704
New France continues its terrorist raids on New England's frontier villages, including Deerfield, Massachusetts.

1710
Col. Francis Nicholson escorts four Mohawk chiefs to London to plead with Queen Anne for naval support. Nicholson then captures Port Royal.

1712
A plan to attack Montreal fails when English ships abandon Nicholson and return to England.

1713
Queen Anne's War ends with the Treaty of Utrecht. England keeps control over Acadia, while the rest of Canada remains French.

1719-1744
Fort Louisbourg is constructed on Cape Breton Island, at the mouth of the St. Lawrence River.

1744
King George's War between France and England begins in North America.

1745
William Pepperell of Massachusetts leads colonial troops to a surprising capture of Louisbourg.

1748
The Treaty of Aix-la-Chapelle ends King George's War. Louisbourg is returned to France.

1754
The French and Indian War has its undeclared beginning.

1755

The English create a four-part plan to prevent New France from expanding: capture of Forts Duquesne, Niagara, and Beausejour (Acadia), and construction of Forts Edward and William Henry; English general Edward Braddock leads his troops into ambush and defeat by the French and their Indian allies in the Battle of the Wilderness; In the Battle of Lake George, William Johnson's colonial troops capture French commander Dieskau and prevent French expansion in the Champlain Valley.

1756

The French and Indian War between England and France is formally declared.

1757

The Marquis de Montcalm is sent to command the French forces in North America. He captures and destroys two English forts: Oswego on Lake Erie and William Henry on Lake George; Fort Beausejour in Acadia is seized by the English, but larger English expeditions to capture Louisbourg and Fort Niagara are abandoned; William Pitt becomes prime minister in

England. His grand plan to defeat France includes the capture of Louisbourg, and Forts Ticonderoga and Duquesne. All English forces are then to converge on the final target, Quebec.

1758

Gen. Jeffrey Amherst leads the English to victory over Louisbourg; French general Montcalm successfully defends Fort Ticonderoga against an English assault; English colonel John Bradstreet captures Fort Frontenac and carries the fort's supplies to the site of Oswego, on Lake Ontario; Easton treaty is signed between the Pennsylvania colonial government and the Delawares, settling boundary questions; As General Forbes marches on Fort Duquesne with English troops, the fort is abandoned and burned by the French. The English begin construction of Fort Pitt on the site.

1759

William Johnson's troops capture Fort Niagara; General Amherst attacks the forts at Ticonderoga and Crown Point; the French abandon and blow up both forts; Quebec is captured by the English.

1760

Governor Vaudreuil of New France surrenders Montreal and all of New France to the combined forces of generals Amherst and William Johnson; Fort Detroit surrenders to Col. Robert Rogers.

1763

Chief Pontiac leads the Indian nations of the Northwest Territory (Indiana, Illinois, Michigan, Ohio) against the English; The Proclamation Act of 1763 is announced by the English government to keep colonial settlers from moving into Indian territory west of the Appalachian Mountains; The Peace of Paris officially ends the French and Indian War between France and England.

1 Old Enemies Meet in a New World

One hundred years after Columbus sailed from Spain into the unknown waters of the Americas, two powerful empires were competing for control of the North American continent: France and England. This war played itself out in the dramatic battle campaigns of the French and Indian War, which began in 1754, was declared in 1756, and ended in 1763. The story of this struggle is rooted in the earliest journeys of French and English explorers into the mysterious new world of North America.

England's first exploration of North America occurred in 1497 when John Cabot left Bristol, England, and arrived on the coast of Canada, probably at present-day Newfoundland. Cabot hoped to find a "northwest passage" through North America to the tea, spices, and silk of Japan and China. Although Cabot was unsuccessful in his search, he was instrumental in exciting an interest in the land itself among the English who followed him. In 1614, for example, Capt. John Smith charted much of

John Cabot stakes his claim to North American territory. His fifteenth-century voyage inspired the English to further explore this mysterious new world.

Samuel de Champlain, Explorer

In 1609 French explorer Samuel de Champlain traveled into the interior of present-day New York State through the valley of a great lake. In "The Voyages to the Great River St. Lawrence (1608-1612)," found in The Heath Anthology of American Literature, *he reported his observations to the French government.*

"There are also many rivers falling into [Lake Champlain], bordered by many fine trees of the same kinds as those we have in France, with many vines finer than any I have seen in any other place; also many chestnut-trees on the border of this lake, which I had not seen before. There is also a great abundance of fish, of many varieties; among others, one called by the savages of the country Chaousarou ["garpike"], which varies in length, the largest being, as the people told me, eight or ten feet long. I saw some five feet long, which were as large as my thigh; the head being as big as my two fists, with a snout two feet and a half long, and a double row of very sharp and dangerous teeth.

Continuing our course over [Lake Champlain] on the western side, I noticed, while observing the country, some very high mountains [the Adirondacks] on the eastern side, on the top of which there was snow. I made inquiry of the savages whether these localities were inhabited. They told me that the Iroquois dwelt there, and that there were beautiful valleys in these places, with plains productive in grain, such as I had eaten in this country, together with many kinds of fruit without limit. . . . After reaching the end of the lake, we should have to go, they said, two leagues by land, and pass through a river [the Hudson] flowing into the sea on the Norumbegue [North American] coast."

the Atlantic coastline for the English from present-day Virginia up to the tip of Maine. From his abundant notes, he took back to his countrymen an enthusiastic call to leave England and settle in the New World.

Here nature and liberty affords us that freely, which in *England* we want, or it costeth us dearely. What pleasure can

be more then, being tired with any occasion a-shore, in planting Vines, Fruits, or Hearbs . . . to recreate themselves before [one's] owne doores, in [one's] owne boates upon the Sea.

Men, woman, and childe, with a small hooke, and line, by angling [fishing], may take [all] sorts of excellent fish, at their pleasures. He is a very bad fisher [that] cannot kill in one day with his hooke and line, one, two, or three hundred Cods.

If a man worke but three dayes in seaven, he may get more then he can spend, unless he will be excessive. . . .

Heere by their labour they may live exceeding well: provided alwaies that first there bee a sufficient power to command them, houses to receive them, meanes to defend them, and provisions for them . . . it is most necessarie to have a fortresse.[1]

Captain Smith was not alone in giving an account of the bounty and beauty of America. During the 1500s, explorers also came from Spain, Portugal, Italy, Sweden, the Netherlands, and France. They were captivated by the promises of wealth they saw in the vast continent across the At-

lantic. By the late 1600s, however, only France and England remained in competition for most of North America. Spain controlled Florida and some territory in the Southwest (now New Mexico and Arizona), but was not a strong threat to the English or French colonies to the north.

The Growth of the English Colonies

English settlers moved in great numbers into the coastal harbors of North America, choosing the locations most likely to support fishing and commerce, farms and towns. English colonists settled in America generally for religious and business reasons. Some of the earliest settlers in New

English colonists walk to church. English colonists generally settled in North America hoping to develop Christian communities along the seaboard.

How Many Native Americans?

Gary Nash, in Red, White and Black, *points out that until recently, reports of the number of Native Americans occupying the New World have been very misleading.*

"On the eve of European contact, how many Native Americans inhabited North America? Until a few years ago, the accepted population of all Native Americans north of Mexico was one million.

It is now believed that the population north of Mexico may have been as high as 10 million. We are left with the startling realization that Europeans were not coming to a 'virgin wilderness,' as some called it. They were invading a land which in some areas was as densely populated as their homelands.

Domed wigwams of birch and elm, copied in the early years by Europeans, were clustered together in villages which were often palisaded (protected by high fences). The extent of development among these Eastern Woodlands societies is indicated by the archaeological evidence of a Huron town in the Great Lakes region. It contained more than one hundred large structures housing a total population of between four and six thousand. Settlements of this size were larger than the average European village of the 16th century. They were also larger than all but a handful of European colonial towns in America."

According to some historians, the Native American population at the time of European contact may have been close to 10 million.

England wanted to develop Christian communities along the seaboard. In 1630 John Winthrop, first governor of Boston, wrote in his essay, "A Model of Christian Charity," the following declaration:

> For the worke wee have in hand it is by a mutuall consent through a speciall overruling providence . . . the Lord will be our God and delight to dwell among us, as his owne people. [He] will command a blessing upon us in all our wayes, soe that wee shall see much more of his wisdome, power, goodness and truthe. . . .
>
> Wee shall finde that the God of Israell is among us, when tenn of us shall be able to resist a thousand of our enemies, when hee shall make us a prayse and glory, that men shall say of succeeding plantacions: the Lord make us like that of New England; for wee must Consider that wee shall be a Citty upon a Hill, the eyes of all people are uppon us.[2]

By 1634, about 10,000 English immigrants had relocated to the New England colonies, which were settled by different political and religious groups. Each English colony governed itself and was responsible for defending itself, even though it was under the control of the English crown.

Although each colony remained independent of the others, the colonies all shared common European attitudes. One such attitude was the conviction that land that had not been "improved," or developed into permanent farms and towns, was wilderness and thus available for the taking. This basic philosophy of ownership and development became the core of conflict between the English colonies and their

Early Europeans, like these Dutch settlers, came to North America with the belief that all undeveloped land could be claimed as their own.

Indian neighbors. Governor Winthrop expressed this philosophy clearly:

> As for the Natives in New England, they inclose noe Land, neither have any setled habytation [dwelling], nor any tame Cattle to improve the Land by. Soe [they] have noe other but a Naturall Right to those Countries. Soe as if we leave them sufficient for their use, we may lawfully take the rest, there being more than enough for them and us.[3]

Thus, English settlers went about building and living on land—shaping former Indian territory into permanent settlements.

French Explorations

France claimed land in the New World in a very different way. Compared to England, France was in a state of relative economic decline. Unlike its neighbors—Spain, Portugal, and the Netherlands—the French court was not able to finance extensive explorations. Consequently, France was among the last of the European powers to investigate North America. It was also less interested in sponsoring and maintaining expensive permanent settlements. Instead, the French preferred to exploit the natural resources they found.

The earliest important French exploration of the New World occurred almost forty years after Cabot's first voyage.

Cartier stands among Native Americans as he claims North American territory for France.

Jacques Cartier's ships ascend the St. Lawrence River as Cartier searches for riches in the New World.

Jacques Cartier, who arrived at the mouth of the St. Lawrence River in 1534, began to search all the way to the Great Lakes for "gold and other riches." Instead he discovered another vast source of natural wealth—fish, and skins from the animals populating that wintry region.

By 1600, France had become England's strongest competitor in the race for riches in the New World. Samuel de Champlain sailing for France in 1608, penetrated deep into North America by way of the St. Lawrence River. During his four years of exploration, he noted the advantages of the great 500-mile-long waterway. From this first voyage, Samuel de Champlain reported:

> We set out on the next day [July 13, 1609], continuing our course in the river as far as the entrance of the lake [Ontario]. There are many pretty islands, here, low, and containing very fine woods and meadows, with

abundance of fowl and such animals of the chase as stags, fallow-deer, roebucks, bears, and others, which go from the main land to these islands. We captured a large number of these animals. There are also many beavers, not only in this river, but also in numerous other little ones that flow into it. These regions, although they are pleasant, are not inhabited by any sav-

A Huron Creation Story

Europeans at first did not think the peoples native to the New World had a religion. Each cultural group, however, had its own well-developed spiritual beliefs. Here is part of the Huron story of creation, "The Woman Who Fell from the Sky," retold by Virginia Hamilton in her collection of creation stories from around the world, In the Beginning.

"In the beginning, there was only water and the water animals that lived in it. Then a woman fell from a torn place in the sky. She was a divine woman, full of power. Two loons flying over the water saw her falling.

The loons held her up and cried for help. They could be heard for a long way as they called for other animals to come.

The snapping turtle came to help. The loons put the woman on the turtle's back. Then the turtle called all the other animals to aid in saving the divine woman's life.

The animals decided the woman needed earth to live on.

Turtle said, 'Dive down in the water and bring up some earth.' Toad went under the water. He stayed too long, and he nearly died. But when Turtle looked inside Toad's mouth, he found a little earth. The woman took it and put it all around on Turtle's shell. That was the start of the earth.

Dry land grew until it formed a country, then another country, and all the earth. To this day, Turtle holds up the earth.

Time passed, and the divine woman had twin boys. They were opposites, her sons. One was good, and one was bad. One was born as children are usually born, in a normal way. But the other one broke out of his mother's side, and she died.

When the divine woman was buried, all of the plants needed for life on earth sprang from the ground above her. From her head came the pumpkin vine. Maize came from her chest. Pole beans grew from her legs."

ages, on account of their wars; but they withdraw as far as possible from the rivers into the interior, in order not to be suddenly surprised.[4]

On a trip into the interior in 1609, Champlain scaled the cliffs of a natural stronghold along the St. Lawrence. There he built a fort he named Quebec, which was destined to become the hub of New France and the focus of English fears. Champlain also developed trade relations with the Huron and Algonquin tribes along the river. He then began to move further into the heavily forested interior along the Richelieu River to a splendid long lake. Thereafter named Lake Champlain, this body of water separates what is now Vermont from upstate New York.

Wherever French explorers went, trappers and traders followed. They took advantage of the enormous treasury of natural resources in fish and fur-bearing

Samuel de Champlain (above) developed trade relations with Native American tribes he encountered along the St. Lawrence River such as the Huron Indians (left).

game. French trappers already monopolized the market in animal skins. French fishermen exported to Europe tons of salted and dried cod and other North Atlantic fish.

In addition, rugged French missionaries often forged deep into the wilderness to tell the Indians about Christianity and to establish French footholds in the new land. By living among their potential converts and not claiming ownership of the land, these priests were instrumental in winning the confidence of the native people. These relationships became important when trappers wanted to come to agreements with the Indians over hunting and trapping rights. Because of their courage, medicinal skills, and loyalty to their converts, the French Roman Catholic priests often attained leadership roles in the tribes. Whenever war broke out between the English and the French, the priests encouraged the Indians to honor their alliances with the French.

French and English Settlements

Because the land was covered with unending dense thickets, swamps, mountains, and forests, there were no roads and travel was much easier and quicker by river than by road. The major French trade routes extended down the logical ribbon of rivers winding through the center of the great continent. Each river reaches out to another lake or river to become a powerful moving highway. The Richelieu River extends south from the St. Lawrence to Lake Champlain and Lake George. From Lake

A French trapper rests with an Indian hunter after a day's hunt. The French easily reached agreements with the Indians over hunting and trapping rights thanks to the rapport between the early French missionaries and the Indians.

George, it was only a short overland journey, or portage, to the junction of the Mohawk River, which enters from the west into the Hudson River. The Hudson then flows south and empties into the Atlantic.

Farther west along the St. Lawrence, canoes traveled through Lakes Ontario and Erie. From Lake Erie, traders portaged south to the upper reaches of the Ohio River. They could then float downstream on the Ohio and Mississippi rivers to the vital French stronghold at New Orleans, established in 1718. By 1682, the French explorer Robert de La Salle had traveled along that great circling necklace of water from Canada to New Orleans. He claimed the entire Mississippi River valley for France, naming it Louisiana in honor of his king, Louis XIV.

To protect France's fur trade routes, Louis XIV commanded that forts be built along the vital connections in the Champlain Valley and through the Ohio River country as well. The forts guarded the waterway from the St. Lawrence in the far north to the mouth of the Mississippi in the far south.

Robert de La Salle claims part of the New World for France, calling the area Louisiana in honor of the French king, Louis XIV.

Busy Towns and Seaports

While the French were building forts at strategic points along the rivers, the English were settling most of the best harbors on the Atlantic seacoast. They created busy towns and seaports, their populations moving steadily into Indian territory along the coast. Because of these permanent settlements, English relations with Native Americans were much more strained than those of the French. The English directly competed for land and resources with tribes located north of Boston and all the way down to New Amsterdam (New York). The Abenaki, Penobscot, Passamaquoddy, Massachusett, Wampanoag, Pequot, Nipmuck, Narragansett, Niantic, and Mahican peoples lived in stable villages on this land. They had all farmed or hunted and fished peaceably for years before the English arrived. However, these tribes were unable to prevent the expansion of the English colonies into the forests and river valleys far from the coast.

The French also had coastal settlements, but they were clustered in "Acadia," a region of sparsely populated farms

French and Indian hunters travel together through rustic terrain. Since the French did not set up colonial boundaries or seize land from the natives for large farms, they were able to live peaceably with the coastal tribes.

and fishing villages established in the early 1600s around the southern entrance of the St. Lawrence River. Occupying today's Nova Scotia, New Brunswick, and Newfoundland, and parts of northern Maine, Acadia was also home to the Abenaki Indians. The Abenakis felt little threat from the French who settled in Acadia because, unlike the English, the French did not set up colonial boundaries and seize land from the natives for large farms. Rather, since the growing season was short along the coast, the Acadians depended on food shipments from France to supplement their little gardens. Thus the French were on relatively friendly terms with the coastal tribes and the native people who hunted in the forests and traveled the rivers. On the other hand, the Acadians never lived peaceably with the English to their south. Similarly, the English colonists never felt safe with the French Acadian settlements on their doorstep.

In the battle to protect their investments in the New World, both the French and the English formed alliances with native tribes. The French sought the help of the Huron and Algonquin people, traditional enemies of the powerful Iroquois, who lived in the upstate New York region.

The English, however, had been able to form an alliance with the Iroquois as a result of a treaty with Holland: the Dutch had maintained a trade agreement with the Iroquois, and the terms were passed on to the English.

English Advantages

When bloodshed between the French and English in North America began, the English had a number of advantages over the French. For example, the alliance between the English and the Iroquois was soon to take on crucial importance; although the French and Indian War, as this conflict is defined today, was not to open until the mid-1700s, hostilities with France in fact began in 1689.

The League of the Iroquois consisted of five Indian nations: Seneca, Cayuga, Onondaga, Oneida, and Mohawk. The members had signed a peace agreement among themselves in the 1500s after many years of tribal warfare. The league had created a strongly united government of equals. In 1713 another native nation, the Tuscarora, joined the league, which now became the Six Nations of the Iroquois. With the powerful Iroquois guarding their western boundaries, the English colonists felt safer and stronger.

Second, England, being stronger than France as a naval power, was able to protect the American coastline. Third, the English settlers outnumbered French settlers ten to one. Thus English colonists would be available to take up arms and fight to protect their territory and trade from French attacks. A fourth advantage England could claim was a better trade system, which yielded more wealth to finance a war.

Dutch settlers trade European goods with Native Americans.

French Advantages

France, on the other hand, was confident of its superiority over England. Its extensive system of forts in key locations throughout the St. Lawrence and Great Lakes regions was one advantage. Moreover, the tightly controlled government of New France answered only to the king, Louis XIV, unlike the English colonies with their independent local governments and self-interests. Changes in French battle plans and troop leadership could be ordered, and general staff could be sure they would be made. The French had also maintained a network of strong Indian alliances, from the Abenakis in Maine to the Algonquins in Wisconsin. Another advantage came in the form of countless French trappers, hunters, and traders, who were at home with the forests and rivers where much of the fighting would take place over the next seventy years. France also took pride in its huge army at home, the strongest standing army in all of Europe. If necessary, many French troops could be sent to fight New World battles.

In reality, neither France nor England had a clear advantage over the other. The wars in North America between these two powers that began in 1689 would take thousands of French, English, and Native American lives before coming to an end more than seventy years later.

Chapter

2 Spreading Flames

Before the French and Indian War began in 1754, several wars between France and England occurred in North America. However, each of these earlier conflicts actually began in Europe. The first war in the series started in 1689 when King Louis XIV attempted to extend France's boundaries by invading a little piece of present-day Germany. England's King William III responded to the invasion by persuading the Dutch and the Austrians to join him in an alliance. Together they declared war on France to force a return of the disputed land.

King William's War

This contest, called the War of the League of Augsburg in Europe, did not remain there. It soon moved to North America, just as all the wars between France and England in the 1600s and 1700s eventually did. Called King William's War in the New World, the fighting involved France's and England's Native American alliances. While the Huron, Algonquin, and Abenaki supported the French, the League of the Iroquois favored the English. If the two colonial powers were to win wars in the New World, they needed to protect and strengthen their alliances with the tribes.

England's King William III declared war against the French in 1689, igniting a fierce eight-year war in North America known as King William's War.

It was during King William's War, 1689-1697, that a French nobleman, the Marquis de Frontenac, developed a style of warfare that had a severe and lingering effect. Louis de Frontenac had been sent by King Louis XIV to direct the war in North America against England. Instead of planning formal battles against English armies, however, Frontenac encouraged a strategy featuring terrorist attacks on small

The Marquis de Frontenac's terrorist tactics created a climate of fear throughout New England.

outlying English villages. Besides burning the villages, French and Abenaki or Caughnawaga Mohawk invaders either killed the residents or carried them off to Canada as captives.

The captives were claimed by either French or Indian families. Once families or friends had paid a ransom, which helped to finance the French war efforts, the captives usually were returned to their homes. Prominent captives were sometimes exchanged for French officers who had been captured by the English.

The raids sponsored by Frontenac created a climate of fear throughout New England. They stiffened English hatred of the French in general and the Roman Catholic church in particular. The English resented the French Catholic missionaries, seeing them as a powerful force in encouraging the Native Americans to fight against the Protestant English. Many a Puritan preacher warned against devious priests who would destroy the Protestant beliefs of anyone carried into captivity. Daniel Sanders, a historian writing in 1812, revealed his interpretation of these feelings:

Indians fighting for the French march with their English captives. Captives were usually held for ransom to help finance France's war efforts.

Indian Complaints

Printed as a tiny volume in 1812, A History of the Indian Wars with the First Settlers of the United States, Particularly in New England, *by Daniel Sanders, tells the story of frontier trials from both the colonists' and Native Americans' viewpoints.*

"[In 1698] the French in their neighborhood often encroaching on territories, the jurisdiction of which was warmly contested, were pressing the savages to new acts of hostilities. The Indians themselves remembered the past with indignation. [They were] full of apprehensions for the future, and already felt grievances not easily to be endured.

They complained that the tribute of corn was not paid them according to stipulation. Their rivers had been obstructed by dams and seines [fishing nets set into the rivers]. Their standing corn had been devoured by the cattle belonging to the white people.

Patents had been granted covering lands, of which they alone were the legitimate owners; to part with which they had neither been asked, nor had they given their assent. [I]n trade the most abusive frauds had been practiced upon them. No attention was paid to complaints not backed by power."

The Indians themselves had begun to adopt the prejudices of the French, and were charmed with [Roman Catholicism]. They had learned to call the English protestants, "heretics;" and of course, believed it was right to destroy the enemies of God. Their opinions rendered them far more cruel than ever. A bounty was also given for English scalps; and the prisoners, sold as slaves, or redeemed by their friends, now became the most profitable articles of merchandize.[5]

Some of the captives chose to remain and even marry within their new culture, to the horror of Protestant New Englanders.

Others who were ransomed wrote accounts of their trials that were widely distributed and read. These "captivity narratives" shaped much of the thinking and resistance in the English colonies. They reinforced negative stereotypes of Indians and Catholics, while at the same time displaying Protestant ideals of behavior and belief.

Massachusetts Strikes Back

The English colonies developed a strategy to respond to the terrifying attacks by the French and their Indian allies. Just as Quebec was the center of French authority and action, Boston was the hub of the New England colonies. Out of Boston came the first of several historic efforts to eliminate the French threat to the English colonies. Both Quebec and Acadia were the early targets, for they were seen as the sources of the French raids. In *History of the Indian Wars*, Daniel Sanders noted the conflict over Acadia:

> Acadie, the ancient name of Nova Scotia, was possessed by the French. . . . The English and French nations, long before this, had entertained towards each other strong jealousies of each other's growing power, feeling the most implacable resentments, which time served rather to increase then to extinguish. The French, residing in Acadie, resembled the natives in their habits and mode of living much more than the English did.[6]

Since Port Royal was the most important French settlement in Acadia, it was a logical target during King William's War. William Phips, mariner and adventurer, received approval from colonial authorities in Massachusetts to lead an expedition to capture Port Royal in 1690. The small French garrison there fell easily. Upon returning to Boston, Phips heard that New

French colonists and Indians revel together at Port Royal. As the most important French settlement in Acadia, Port Royal became the target of English attack.

York colonists were planning an overland assault on Quebec. Encouraged by his success at Port Royal, Phips saw hope in a two-pronged attempt to take Quebec. An overland expedition up the Champlain Valley in New York would meet a naval expedition sailing up the St. Lawrence River at Quebec. While the New Yorkers organized the land campaign, Phips gathered an assortment of fishing and merchant vessels for the naval assault on the Rock, as Quebec was called.

What followed was hardly what the confident Phips had anticipated. The overland expedition never reached Quebec, and Phips's naval challenge to the Rock was treated as a nuisance by the governor of New France. More than a century later, historian Samuel Adams Drake summarized the results of the effort by Phips and his forces:

Phips' naval attempt was ushered in by bluster. After getting his fleet up the St. Lawrence to the great basin before Quebec, no mean feat by itself as the navigation of parts of the St. Lawrence was very tricky, he sent an officer to Frontenac to demand the surrender of the city within one hour. The written summons and a watch were insolently handed to the fiery governor in front of his staff. Instead of the expected explosion, Frontenac for a wonder restrained his temper and returned a courteous but peremptory refusal. There is little need to detail the fumbling attacks that Phips made—they amounted to nothing. His ammunition soon became well nigh exhausted, and both his men and his ships suffered considerably from the fire of the French. . . .

No such terrible humiliation had ever before visited New England. Yet, alone and single-handed, [the colonists] had struck the blow which

---

Anger over French Raids

In The Border Wars of New England, *historian Samuel Adams Drake summarized the outrage the New Englanders felt over the raids led by the French during Queen Anne's War.*

"Of all the trials arising from [Queen Anne's] war, perhaps the hardest to bear was the suspense relative to the fate of friends or relatives. That innocent women and children should be held for ransom was perhaps one of the penalties attached to carrying on a war with barbarians. That a people like the French, professing to represent in themselves the highest type of Christian civilization, should sanction such a practice, was not only fostering one of the worst features of the war, but to all intents it was descending to the level of the savages themselves."

was to be the key-note of future operations against Canada.[7]

In spite of the failed Quebec venture, Phips managed to salvage some small victory by blockading the St. Lawrence. The blockade, made possible by his Acadian victory at Port Royal, prevented relief ships from France from getting through to Quebec with food and supplies. The citizens living on the Rock faced a winter of hardship and famine.

Pleas to London for help with the "languishing and exhausting" war produced no aid for Massachusetts. When King William III agreed to end the war in Europe in 1697, very little was resolved for the New World. In the Treaty of Ryswick, Acadia was officially returned to France. No one in New England felt that any of the territorial disputes had been settled. King William died in 1698, and as the next British monarch, Queen Anne, began her reign, the New England colonies were weary and fearful.

Queen Anne's War

The colonists' fears were not exaggerated, for after a few years of peace, war between France and England broke out again in the New World. The hostilities between French and English colonies grew larger, and the attacks and defenses became grander in scale. Yet the strategies and goals remained the same: to claim and control as much of North America as possible.

The war that has come to be known as Queen Anne's War, like King William's War, was in fact a product of the expansionary aims of Louis XIV, the king of

Queen Anne holds the scepter and orb, symbols of her power.

France. When Charles II, the king of Spain, died without leaving an heir, Louis saw a perfect opportunity to unite France and Spain by having his grandson Philip succeed Charles on the Spanish throne. England's Queen Anne was determined to prevent such an event. She immediately joined Austria and other European powers in declaring war on France. The European phase of the War of the Spanish Succession began in 1701, and by 1703 the hostilities had spread to North America, under the name of "Queen Anne's War."

The war's ten-year impact was felt primarily in Massachusetts. The French concentrated their attacks on New England to avoid angering the Iroquois in New York. Although Frontenac had died, terrorist raids on frontier English villages began again and increased in frequency. A typical example was the French and Abenaki attack that overwhelmed the stockaded village of Deerfield, Massachusetts, on February 29, 1704. The village, set in the fields of the fertile Connecticut River valley, was burned almost to destruction. The raiders forced 111 captives to make the long winter march to Canada.

Such raids were designed to intimidate the New England colonies into pulling back their settlements instead of trying to expand them. Mohawk allies of the French were rewarded with captives to use as servants or as replacements for dead

English colonists defend themselves against brutal French and Indian raids.

Rev. John Williams was a prestigious figure in the Deerfield village. French and Indian attackers captured Williams during the savage Deerfield raid, hoping his high status would bring a large ransom.

Redeemed Captive, Returning to Zion, he wrote about those remaining behind:

> We have reason to bless God who has wrought deliverance for so many, and yet to pray to God for a door of escape to be opened for the great number yet behind, not much short of a hundred, many of which are children. Of these not a few [are] among the savages and having lost the English tongue [forgotten how to speak English], will be lost and turn savages in a little time unless something extraordinary prevent [this from happening].
>
> [But] through God's goodness we all arrived in safety at Boston November twenty-one [1706], the number of captives fifty-seven, two of which were my children. I have yet [captive] a daughter of ten years of age and many neighbors whose case bespeaks your compassion and prayers to God to Gather them, being outcasts ready to perish.[8]

A number of the Deerfield children never returned to Massachusetts, including Reverend Williams's daughter, Eunice, who was ten years old at the time of the raid. Eunice not only preferred to remain in Canada, she married into the Caughnawaga branch of the Mohawk tribe. From *The Border Wars of New England*, published in 1897, comes this summary of the destiny of most of the Deerfield captives, including Eunice Williams:

> After suffering untold hardships, the surviving captives [of the Deerfield attack] straggled into the Indian villages on the St. Lawrence. Some sixty were eventually restored to their friends, a few at a time, either by ransom or

family members. The Abenaki also fought to avenge a massacre by the English of a gathering of Abenaki leaders in an area of Massachusetts that is now part of Maine. The raids provided income and a sense of power to the French, since they received ransom money for many of the captives.

The most prestigious Deerfield captive was the village minister, Rev. John Williams. In the early Puritan years in New England, the Protestant clergyman, or minister, was the most important leader in a town. As a captive, then, a minister would bring the largest ransom from family and New England church authorities. Williams returned home in 1706. In *The*

A Captive's Story

Rev. John Williams told the story of his captivity in The Redeemed Captive, Returning to Zion, *published in 1707. In this excerpt, the clergyman relates the trials of the winter journey to Canada.*

"In our fourth day's march the enemy killed another of my neighbors, who being nigh the time of travail, was wearied with her journey. When we came to the great river [the Connecticut], the enemy took sleighs to draw their wounded, several of our children, and their packs, and marched a great pace. I traveled many hours in water up to the ankles. Near night I was very lame, having before my travel wronged my ankle bone and sinews; I thought, so did others, that I should not be able to hold out to travel far. I lifted up my heart to God (my only refuge) to remove my lameness and carry me through with my children and neighbors if He judged it best; however, I desired God would be with me in my great change if He called me by such a death to glorify Him. And that He would take care of my children and neighbors and bless them, and within a little space of time I was well of my lameness to the joy of my children and neighbors, who saw so great an alteration in my traveling.

My feet were very sore, and each night I wrung blood out of my stockings when I pulled them off . . . by the goodness of God, I never wanted a meal's meat during my captivity, though some of my children and neighbors were greatly wounded (as I may say) with the arrows of famine and pinching want, having for many days nothing but roots to live upon and not much of them either. My master gave me a piece of a Bible, never disturbed me in reading the Scriptures, or in praying to God."

A captured Deerfield family endures the long winter march to Canada.

exchange. Eunice, [Reverend Williams's] . . . daughter, was adopted by the Caughnawaga tribe, embraced the Catholic faith, and eventually married a full-blooded Caughnawaga Indian named Amrusus, who thenceforth appears to have taken his wife's family name of Williams.[9]

The Deerfield event reinforced in New Englanders the belief that the Indians were ruthless savages, even though the Abenaki attackers had been acting for the French. Each raid was composed of a large number of Indians with a small number of French, and the Indians received most of the blame. Historian Samuel Adams Drake summarized this attitude:

The Rev. Solomon Stoddard, minister of Northampton [near Deerfield], . . . declared that the Indians should be looked upon only as "thieves and murderers." He proposed hunting them down with dogs "the same as we do bears.". . . There is no doubt whatever that he spoke the general opinion [in western Massachusetts]. At that very moment his own flock were anxiously discussing the chances of having the Indians come down upon them without a moment's warning. Then again the atrocities of [King William's War] were now freshly recalled with fear and trembling; hardly one family could be found, along a wide extent of border, not mourning the loss of a relative or a friend. The morality of any effectual method of retaliation was not likely to be called in question. . . .

The Massachusetts government [offered] a bounty of twenty pounds for every Indian scalp, . . . thus to authorize the forming of scalping parties. This put those engaging in them on a level with the savages themselves. Yet public feeling had reached a point when no more was thought of killing an Indian than a wolf.[10]

Attacks on New France

In 1709 a plan came out of Boston to put an end to French terrorism. Col. Francis Nicholson was chosen to strike at New France through a naval attack on Acadia. Similar to William Phips's ill-fated effort during King William's War, the naval attack was to be combined with an inland expedition. This time, however, English forces would move down Lake Champlain to Montreal, an easier target than the Rock of Quebec.

An experienced politician with little military training, Nicholson nevertheless realized that a successful campaign would require numerous ships and troops. In a brilliant move, Nicholson appealed to England's faithful allies, the Canajoharie Mohawks, for help. Nicholson persuaded four Mohawk chiefs to accompany him to London in 1709 to plead with Queen Anne to support the effort against France. The dramatic appearance of the chiefs, in their native splendor, stunned the English court. The Mohawks' impressive speech on behalf of Nicholson's plan convinced the queen to fund the expedition. Full-length portraits of the chiefs were painted by prominent English society painters, and engravings of the portraits became very popular among wealthy Londoners.

A year later, five small English warships with 400 troops landed in Boston. Nicholson organized local volunteers to join him in an attack on Port Royal in Acadia, which had been returned to the French in 1697. Fortunately for Nicholson, Port Royal was lightly manned and barely able to defend itself. After a brief formal exchange of cannon fire, the fort's commander requested an honorable surrender. Nicholson was delighted to accommodate the enemy, allowing the small band to leave the fort with drums beating and flags flying.

The surrender of Port Royal in 1710 helped sway the queen's court to accept the final stage of Nicholson's plan, a joint naval and land attack on Montreal. In 1712 Nicholson himself led the troops into the interior and down the Champlain Valley. The queen's fleet of fifteen warships and forty transport ships carrying 12,000 troops was ready to sail. Surely the defeat of New France was finally in reach. In late autumn, Nicholson and his troops set out for Montreal, expecting to join the English fleet on the St. Lawrence River outside Montreal. But the grand assault was not to be. Admiral Walker, commander of the naval assault, lost ten ships on the dangerous rocks at the entrance of the St. Lawrence. He then gave up the effort, and the fleet returned to England. Nicholson and his troops were left stranded in the Champlain Valley, without crucial

Defeated Acadians evacuate Port Royal after their surrender to English troops.

English Puritan Fears of French Catholicism

The English Puritan colonists feared the French Roman Catholics and their Indian allies equally. This illustrative description by a captive from Pemaquid, Maine, in 1689, is recorded in Samuel Adams Drake's book The Border Wars of New England.

"A few days after[ward] we arrived at Penobscot fort, where I again saw my mother, my brother and sisters and many other captives. I think we tarried here eight days. In that time the Jesuit of the place had a great mind to buy me. My Indian master made a visit to the Jesuit, and took me with him. I saw the Jesuit show my master pieces of gold, and understood afterward that he was tendering them for my ransom. He gave me a biscuit, which I put in my pocket, and not daring to eat it, I buried it under a log, fearing he had put something in it to make me love him. When my mother heard the talk of my being sold to a Jesuit, she said to me, 'Oh, my dear child, if it were God's will, I had rather follow you to your grave, or nevermore see you in this world, than that you should be sold to a Jesuit; for a Jesuit will ruin your body and soul.'"

naval support. The plan to strike New France was in ruins.

Queen Anne's War came to an end in 1713, with the signing of the Treaty of Utrecht. The end of hostilities came more because France's war in Europe was faltering than as a result of any impressive English victory. The defeated king, Louis XIV, was so burdened with war debt that he finally abandoned his New World ambitions and settled for peace. Even so, the English had failed to claim a major victory in North America. Each side received some satisfaction. Acadia was placed under English control, but the French remained in charge of Canada and its major waterways. The Treaty of Utrecht brought peace to the New World for thirty years.

Chapter

3 A Mighty Fortress

The Treaty of Utrecht, signed in 1713, ended Queen Anne's War and brought welcome relief from years of terrifying surprise attacks on English outposts in North America. Whether the peace accord would actually settle territorial questions was unclear, however. The treaty identified only vaguely the land boundaries between New France and the English colonies, both coastal and interior, an uncertainty that guaranteed future conflict.

After the initial relief over the war's end, both the French and English colonies settled into a cold war. The Treaty of Utrecht had brought an end to active warfare, but France and England did not rest. Both enemy nations still intended to enlarge their territorial claims and thereby tilt the balance of power in world affairs to their advantage. The English strengthened their colonies and constructed forts in New England for protection, while the French rebuilt their existing forts and added new ones to guard their widespread territory.

During the three decades that followed the end of Queen Anne's War, the number of English settlers who migrated from Europe to America greatly increased. By 1750, there were more than a million English colonists in America. By comparison only about 50,000 settlers lived in all

of New France. French settlements, however, remained concentrated along the St. Lawrence River, and colonists in New France continued to rely heavily on the mother country for food and provisions. The English colonists carved out prosperous farms, villages, and cities, mostly in New England. English immigrants were rapidly moving inland from the seacoast and looking for even more land to settle.

English Expand Territory

Although most of England's colonial development was located in the northeast, the English nevertheless intended to protect the entire coastline from expansion by the French, who were well established in the Mississippi River valley to the west, and by the Spanish, who occupied the Florida peninsula. The English Parliament approved a plan to develop a "buffer" colony, one that would occupy the land between Florida and the Carolinas. Thus in the early 1730s Gen. James Oglethorpe and other businessmen invested much of their personal fortunes in this new colony, which was called Georgia after George II, the king of England.

Most of the southern territory between the Mississippi River and the Atlantic

Ocean was occupied by a large population of Chickasaw, Creek, and Cherokee Indians. These tribes tried to balance the power between the English and Spanish in their region by negotiating with both sides. In the north, the Six Nations of the Iroquois tried to maintain a balance of power between the French and English. It was clear to the Iroquois, however, that their best hope was to maintain the alliance with the English, since many Canadian tribes strengthened the French. In both the north and the south, the goal of the Native Americans was to keep any one European nation from taking complete control.

While England was settling new colonies during the thirty years of peace, France was equally busy. To protect their interests throughout valleys of the Ohio and Mississippi rivers the French strengthened their system of forts. With the establishment of New Orleans at the mouth of the Mississippi, France controlled a complete water route for trade, from the Gulf of Mexico to the Great Lakes and the St. Lawrence River.

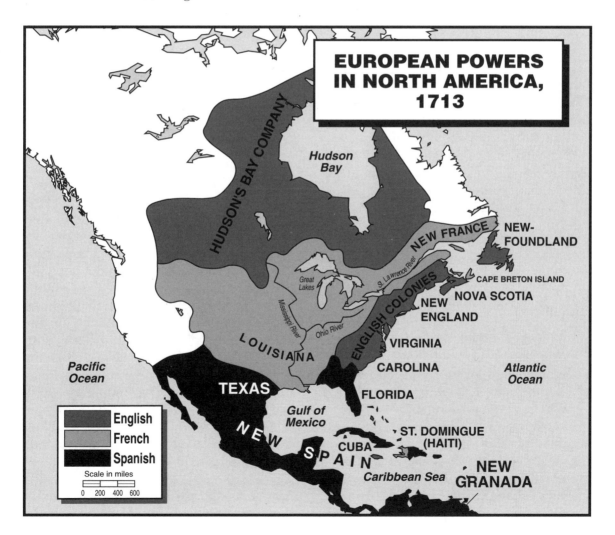

EUROPEAN POWERS IN NORTH AMERICA, 1713

Hudson Bay

HUDSON'S BAY COMPANY

NEW FRANCE

NEW-FOUNDLAND

CAPE BRETON ISLAND

Great Lakes

St. Lawrence River

NOVA SCOTIA

Mississippi River

Ohio River

ENGLISH COLONIES

NEW ENGLAND

LOUISIANA

VIRGINIA

Pacific Ocean

CAROLINA

Atlantic Ocean

TEXAS

FLORIDA

Gulf of Mexico

NEW SPAIN

CUBA

ST. DOMINGUE (HAITI)

NEW GRANADA

Caribbean Sea

English
French
Spanish

Scale in miles
0 200 400 600

Fortress Louisbourg

One of the string of forts built to protect French trade interests was called Louisbourg. The massive granite complex overlooked the Atlantic Ocean on Cape Breton Island, Nova Scotia, at the extreme eastern point of Canada. Guarding the strategic entrance to the St. Lawrence River, and named for King Louis XIV, Louisbourg was the largest and most impressive of the French forts. Its construction had taken twenty-five years and was not completed during Louis's lifetime.

Louisbourg reinforced French control of the European fur trade and the rich fishing grounds in the North Atlantic. From the interior of the continent, French trappers brought furs to meet the demands for the latest fashions in Paris and brought huge profits to French traders. Sailing out of Louisbourg harbor, hundreds of French fishing boats provided France with three times the volume of mackerel and cod caught by the entire English and American colonial fishing fleets. The fort's location on Cape Breton Island provided important advantages for France, which were noted in detail by a later historian:

> Strangely enough, up to this time little or no attention had been paid to this island. Three or four insignificant fishing ports existed on its coasts, but as yet the whole interior [of New France] was a shaggy wilderness. . . . Such natural productions for the country as masts, boards, ship-timber, flax, hemp, plaster, iron and copper ores, dried fish, whale and seal oils, and salted meats, might be exported . . . provided a suitable port were secured, at once safe, commodious [roomy], and well situated for collecting all these commodities, and shipping them abroad.

> By creating such a port as . . . suggested [at Louisbourg], the voyage from France would be shortened one-half. The dangerous navigation of the St. Lawrence would be altogether avoided. Instead of large ships having to continue their voyages to Quebec, the carrying trade of the St. Lawrence would fall to coasting vessels owned in the colony. A strong hand would also be given to the neighbor province, the fertile yet unprotected Acadia. It might thus be preserved against the designs of the English, while a thriving trade in wines, brandies, linens, and rich stuffs might reasonably be expected to spring up with the neighboring [English] colonies.[11]

Designed by the Marquis de Vauban, the foremost military architect of the age, Louisbourg was sited on a granite outcrop of Cape Breton Island alongside a perfect, sheltered deepwater harbor. Its most striking features were the sculpted stone walls that appeared to extend out of the granite ledge on which they were laid. The lines of the walls had been calculated so that each projection or point of the star-shaped fort extended well out from the center. Each point had space for scores of huge cannon, some of them capable of hurling a sixty-pound lead ball into the sails or hull of an attacking ship. When completed in 1744, Louisbourg appeared to be indestructible.

Taking no chances, however, the French added protection in the form of thirty cannon at the Royal Battery on the shore across from the fort. Another thirty cannon at the Island Battery guarded the mouth of the harbor. The fort itself boasted 400 cannon. With flags flying and its castlelike towers rising above the rocky coast, Louisbourg was a masterpiece of Old World architecture.

An Englishman visiting Louisbourg after 1745 described the fortress:

> The Cittadel [fortification] . . . was a Very Large House. Being 23 Rods Long and about 45 Feet Wide all Built of Stone and Brick. It was defended Having a trench between it and the Citty [civilian village]. The Bridge on which we went over (part of it) was Easily Highsted [drawn] up. In the Middle was A Steeple where Hung an Excellent Bell, the Biggest (By far) that Ever I see. At the East End it is three Stories and Several Larg Rooms Well finished. There is also a Chappel in it Larg Enough to hold Large Congregation. I Trust 1000 Men may Live Comfortably in Said House [barracks].[12]

King George's War

During the years when Louisbourg was being constructed on Cape Breton Island, the people of nearby Acadia lived under the control of the English. Over a period of several generations, the French farmers and fishing families became accustomed to English colonial rule. This peaceful arrangement changed abruptly in 1744, however, when war between France and England broke out again in Europe. After the death of Queen Anne, George II had become king of England. Thus the third

war in North America became King George's War. In Europe it was called the War of Austrian Succession because when Emperor Charles VI died without a male heir [no woman ever ruled the Holy Roman Empire], a vacant throne again became a cause for contention.

As soon as the governor of Louisbourg, the Marquis de Duquesnel, heard about the new war between France and England, he began maneuvers to recover the large tract of land in Acadia for France. Once again, Acadia became the focus for both New France and New England.

Duquesnel tried unsuccessfully to recapture Port Royal, Acadia's capital, from the English in 1744, but his action alarmed New Englanders. Gov. William Shirley of Massachusetts and other New England leaders realized that France

Gov. William Shirley of Massachusetts masterminded the siege at Louisbourg.

Pepperell's Instructions

Gov. William Shirley of Massachusetts masterminded the colonial attack on Louisbourg. Part of the instructions he gave to Sir William Pepperell, commander of the ground forces, are reproduced here as they appear in Raymond F. Baker's paper, "A Campaign of Amateurs," which is part of the Canadian Historic Sites series of catalogues.

"Take care, that the fleet be sure of their distance eastward . . . to prevent their being seen from the town in the day time. In the evening they are to push into the bay, as far at least as to be able to land at . . . Flat Point Cove. As soon as the transports are at an anchor, the troops who must be ready, are to be immediately, by the whale boats, landed in the best manner that haste can allow. Keep the four detachments each together . . . march, following the range and under cover of the hills, round to the north west and north, &c. Till they come to the back of the grand battery (cannon placement).

Here they are also to halt, till a signal agreed on be given, for them to march immediately to the said battery, and attack it. The attack at the grand battery you must order, Sir, by entering at a low part of the wall, that is unfinished at the east end. For which ladders are sent on purpose.

If it be impracticable to think of surprising the town, and you [decide] on the surprise of the grand battery, let the party designed for attacking the grand battery be first landed. Next the party to cover them. You must let this be attempted by a number of whale boats. [You] must land a party of three hundred men, on the back of the island [Cape Breton]. Or in a little well known beachy cove at the south-easterly point, just within the breaking point of rocks, which runs off. From either of which places, in a very calm time they may enter successfully. If so, immediately order a [bombardment], there to play on the town, and garrison the battery, with as many men as you can spare. [They] will be wanted there to fight the guns, in case any enemy should approach afterwards by sea."

could not be allowed to resume harassing English settlements in Acadia and along the northern frontier. The only way to put a stop to this threat was to capture Louisbourg. On the basis of reports from former captives who had been held in the fort, Governor Shirley was convinced that Louisbourg was not indestructible. In a speech to the Massachusetts General Court [legislature], Shirley reasoned:

Nothing would more effectually promote the interests of [Massachusetts] . . . than a reduction of that place [Louisbourg]. . . . From the best information that can be had of the circumstances of the Town and of the number of the soldiers and Militia within it, and of the situation of the Harbour, I have good reason to think that if Two Thousand men were landed upon the Island [Cape Breton] as soon as they may be conveniently got ready . . . such a number of men would, with the blessing of Divine Providence upon their enterprise, be masters of the field at all events.[13]

Shirley tried to keep his plan to attack Louisbourg a secret, except to his own legislators, but somehow word leaked out. The news quickly spread throughout all of New England. Soon the other New England colonies were eager to join Massachusetts in a combined plan to attack Louisbourg.

The First Louisbourg Expedition

Governor Shirley finally assembled a total of ninety boats, most of them small transport vessels, plus a few armed ships. Under the command of Sir William Pepperell, the expedition set sail from Boston on March 24, 1745. The wealthy Pepperell sat on the Governor's Council and had been a militiaman much of his life. Yet it is hard to imagine how the New England colonists could have designed a plot more certain to fail. The troops—approximately 4,500 men with little or no combat experience—were

With his inexperienced troops, Sir William Pepperell launched a surprise attack on Louisbourg.

led by officers who had almost no practical knowledge of making decisions in the frenzy of battle. In addition, many vessels in the small flotilla had been fishing boats a month earlier. A single French battleship could have blown to splinters most of the English fleet in a single broadside hit.

Pepperell managed to land all his troops at Canso on the south end of Cape Breton Island, where he established a base and erected a blockhouse, or fortified watchtower. From there, Pepperell had been instructed by Governor Shirley to launch a surprise attack on Louisbourg; he was to

proceed, with the fleet from Canso, in order to attack the town of Louisbourg, which [it] has been thought may be surprised, if they have no advice of

Stephen Williams's Journal

At ten years of age, Stephen Williams was captured in the French and Abenaki attack on Deerfield during Queen Anne's War. Later he was returned to Massachusetts. This excerpt from Williams's journal as chaplain to Pepperell's forces was published in Louisbourg Journals, 1745 *by Louis DeForest. The entries describe the world political situation and activities during the siege of Louisbourg in 1745.*

"24 August . . . a French priviteer sloop [privately owned one-masted vessel that attacked other ships for personal treasure] came just to the island Battery—but seeing English colours [flag]—stood off—and made to the East and took one of our wood sloops. Capt. Fletcher went after her—but I fear whether he'll be able to find her

4 September citadell and Hospitall—am able to keep about tho but poorly [Williams was quite ill during most of his stay at Louisbourg]. Visited dr pynchon. This day we hear that . . . the duke of Tuscany is chosen Emperour [of Austria-Hungary, thus ending King George's War, known in Europe as the War of the Austrian Succession]. . . . If true as I hope it is. We hear also that a ship was seen off—and we are concerned—not knowing but, they are french

5 September I went up to the citadell—but just then—the drums—were beating, to call to arms. We had an Alarm—a report, being Spread—that two Large Ships appeard in the offing. The companys were called to arms—But the fog came on—that we could see nothing from the walls.

10 . . . toward night we heard that twas thot a french fleet was seen off cape Sables—and therefore, twas agreed the Fleet should go out. At night the men that had listd—were orderd—to be in a readiness to go aboard the Kings ships Early

21 November this day fourty year ago, I arrivd at Boston, from Canada, where I had been a prisoner. Thus the Lord has waitd upon me fourty year—but alas, how often have I Grievd him, and badly abusd his Goodness. The Lord be pleasd graciously to pardon and accept me, for the Sake of j x [Jesus Christ]; amen."

your coming. Your proceedings from Canso must be such as to time your arrival . . . about nine of the clock in the evening, or sooner, or later, as you can best rely on the wind, weather, and darkness of the night.[14]

Once they had sailed quietly past the fortress under cover of darkness, the English flotilla landed in a tiny cove behind the fortress. The first task was to win control of the heavy cannon in and around the harbor, which guarded the main structure. In the dawn's light the next day, the English launched a surprise attack and captured the Royal Battery, the large placement of cannon in the inner harbor. The first stage in capturing the fort itself was completed.

After seizing the Royal Battery, the inexperienced but clever men of Pepperell's ragtag invading force wasted no time. For weeks they manually dragged the enormous cannon from the captured battery, across a stretch of marshland, and up a slope. From there they could fire directly on the fort. To move the huge guns, each weighing tons, as many as 300 men were harnessed to crude sleds, which cradled the weapons. They worked at night, despite fatigue and numbing cold water often up to their knees. Eventually the determined men succeeded in moving enough cannon into position to begin shelling the fort.

Governor Shirley had arranged for the support of three English warships com-

Pepperell surveys his troops as they drag heavy cannon from the captured Royal Battery to their firing position above Louisbourg.

manded by Commodore Peter Warren, who was sympathetic to the New Englanders. These vessels were stationed in the West Indies, however, and did not arrive until almost a month after Pepperell and his men had begun their assault. As soon as Warren and his squadron arrived, they set up a blockade of the harbor. This action prevented any French transports or supply ships from assisting the fortress.

Trapped inside this blockade, the French were isolated, and the New Englanders continued their bombardment.

It was not long before the heavy shot had done its work, and mighty Louisbourg began to crumble. Rev. Stephen Williams, former boy captive and now chaplain to the army, recorded in his journal:

I this day heard of a Say [report] that Morepang [harbor captain of Louis-

---

The Fall of Louisbourg

In The Taking of Louisbourg, 1745, *Samuel Adams Drake, in 1890, recorded the response on both sides of the ocean to the surrender at Louisbourg.*

"The surrender caused great rejoicing in the colonies, as was natural it should, with all except those who had always predicted its failure. For some reason the news did not reach Boston until July 2, in the night. At daybreak the inhabitants were aroused from their slumbers by the thunder of cannon. The whole day was given up to rejoicings. A public thanksgiving was observed on the 18th. The news reached London on the 20th. The Tower guns were fired, and at night London was illuminated. Similar demonstrations occurred in all the cities and large towns of the kingdom.

At Versailles [the French court], the news caused deep gloom. De Luynes speaks of it thus in his Memoirs: 'People have been willing to doubt about this affair of Louisbourg, but unhappily it is only too certain. These misfortunes have given rise to altercations among ministers. It is urged that M. Maurepas [an advisor to Louis XV] is at fault in having allowed Louisbourg to fall for want of munitions. The friends of Maurepas contend that he did all that was possible, but could not obtain the necessary funds from the Treasury.' The government got ready two fleets to retake Louisbourg. One was scattered or sunk by storms in 1746, and one was destroyed . . . in 1747 off Cape Finisterre."

English flags fly triumphantly after the successful English attack on Louisbourg. The victory was a source of great pride to the English colonists.

bourg under the French] had said: that he thot the England men were Cowards—but now he thot that if they had a pick ax and Spade—they would dig their way to Hell and Storm it which they had done.[15]

In his article "A Campaign of Amateurs," Canadian historian Raymond F. Baker summarizes the famous attack and its impact in Europe:

The outcome of the siege both surprised and shocked French officials in Paris, who found it difficult to understand how an amateur army of undisciplined volunteers could capture the "strongest" French fortress in North America. . . . Many [English commentators] attributed success to the will of God, of whom they were the instrument designed to rid the continent of a great "Stronghold of Satan." Others did not know why they had succeeded but thought it was "the most glorious and useful thing done in the war."[16]

Bitter Disappointment

Less than two months after landing, Pepperell's daring amateur army had forced the French to raise a flag of surrender. The elation of the conquest was soon followed by the difficult occupation of Louisbourg by the English colonials, however.

Negro and Indian Soldiers Among Pepperell's Troops

In his journal from July through December 1745, Stephen Williams documents daily the illness and deaths in the English colonial army occupying Louisbourg after its capture in June 1745. This portion of the journal, published in Louisbourg Journals, 1745, *by Louis DeForest, lists the Negro and Indian soldiers in the colonial army that Williams counted as having died at Louisbourg.*

"1. Eastman' Negro London, dyd this morning

2. philip Negro (formerly servant to the Revd mr devotion of Suffd [Suffield] dyd he was of collonell Storers company

3. an indian of Rhodeisland dyd

4. a negro of capt: Westons company [was buried]

5. yesterday an indian of capt: John-sons company dyd

6. this day one merrill a mosheto indian or melatto, of the Generalls regiment dyd

7. an indian of capt: Lawrences company dyd

8. a Negro of cap Rhodes company [died]

9. an indian of capt: Lawrences company [died]

10. a free Negro of capt: Heustons company dyd this day

11. an indian of collonell Richmonds company dyd

12. one Slate an indian of collonell Broadstreets company [buried]

13. Glovers negro, peter, [buried]

14. Newport Cofew a free Negro, of capt: Mountfords company [buried]

15. this morning, John Sassiman, an indian of capt: hathaways company—was found dead, in the street"

The fort was cramped for space, with both French and English troops inside, and provisions were poor. Illness swept through the ranks, and many died.

The conquest of Louisbourg was a great victory for the New Englanders, but their pride turned to bitter disappointment in 1748, when the Treaty of Aix-la-Chapelle returned the prize to France in exchange for Madras, a piece of India the French had seized from the English.

The return of Louisbourg to France was viewed as an insult to the English colonies in North America. King George's War had done little to resolve the conflicts between France and England in the New World. Six years later, war broke out again between these two powerful rivals.

4 Sparks in the Wilderness

Deep in the Ohio wilderness, 200 miles south of Lake Erie, lay a site of strategic importance for both the French and the British. Each targeted it for a fort bearing its flag. This site—the Forks—was located where two key rivers joined to form the vital Ohio River. For the French, the site was vital for protecting the arteries of the Ohio and Mississippi rivers down to French New Orleans. England wanted a fort there to protect its claims to the same region, which had been mapped as part of Virginia territory many years before. The race was on to fortify the Forks.

To protect English interests in the disputed territory of the Ohio Valley, in 1753 Virginia's governor Robert Dinwiddie took action. He sent a red-headed, twenty-one-year-old Virginian named George Washington to protest French construction of two new forts. The twin French forts of Presque Isle and LeBoeuf had been hastily erected. Their positions guarded the portage trade path between

George Washington fords the Allegheny River to deliver a message to the French. As a representative of English interests, Washington protested the construction of French forts in the Ohio Valley region.

Lake Erie and the upper reaches of the Ohio River system. Washington arrived to find the French firmly established with no intention of abandoning their new forts. Governor Dinwiddie realized that the English needed to fortify the Forks as soon as possible. Otherwise, Virginia was in danger of losing its claim on the Ohio Valley. Woodsmen sent to construct a log fort on the site, however, found they were too late. There, flying the French fleur-de-lis [flag symbol], was Fort Duquesne. The French had anticipated Dinwiddie's response and had quickly constructed the third new fort. Washington reassured Dinwiddie that if he could establish a base camp near Duquesne and be given reinforcements, he could capture the fort. With the governor's support, Washington left Alexandria, Virginia, in May 1754. Leading about 120 men, he slashed a rough wagon trail over the Appalachian Mountains and arrived at the Great Meadows, not far from Fort Duquesne.

Washington's small band ambushed a French party near the fort, killing its commander. When this news entered the fort, a strong force of French troops and their Indian allies from the Ohio Valley region emerged to avenge the commander's death. Washington found himself forced to move quickly to protect his troops. With little planning, he and his men built a rude stockade named Fort Necessity. Surrounded by his attackers during a spring downpour, the young Washington lost a third of his men to enemy fire. Fort Necessity was quickly overcome by French attackers, and Washington requested surrender terms. In the noblest European tradition, the French allowed the losers to depart in an orderly, although ragged,

Washington slashes a rough trail through the mountains (right) to establish a garrison from which to capture Fort Duquesne (left).

At Fort Necessity, Washington and his troops plot their strategy against the French. Washington's failure to capture Fort Duquesne and his eventual defeat at Fort Necessity increased tension between the French and English in North America.

fashion from shabby Fort Necessity. The troops slowly made their way back to Virginia by way of their freshly cut path.

George Washington's defeat at Fort Necessity in early summer 1754 turned out to be one of the crucial events in the decades of fighting between France and England in North America. As the English statesman Horace Walpole concluded many years later, "a volley fired by a young Virginian in the backwoods of America set the world on fire."[17] The first strong reactions to the defeat came from the English colonists and Native Americans living in the region near the French forts.

An Urgent Meeting at Albany

Washington's failure to seize Fort Duquesne ignited an undeclared war between France and England in North America. Two years later, a formal declaration of war between the two countries would open the final war between them, the French and Indian War.

With conflict erupting in the Ohio Valley, the English colonies were concerned about protecting themselves. A few months after Washington's surrender on July 4, 1754, eight of the thirteen colonies agreed to send representatives to Albany to talk about working together. Some of the colonial leaders saw an urgent need to unite in some form of loose government, or union. Governor Shirley of Massachusetts remarked to his own colonial assembly:

> For forming this general union, gentlemen, there is no time to be lost: the French seem to have advanced further toward making themselves masters of this Continent within the past five or six years than they have done ever since the first beginning of that settlement.[18]

The Albany Congress of 1754 was an idea of Benjamin Franklin. The Philadelphia statesman and inventor proposed uniting colonial defenses to face the French threat. He also proposed the style of government used by the Iroquois, after having read a history of the Iroquois

Benjamin Franklin urged the colonies to unite to protect themselves from the imposing French forces.

appears [unbreakable]. Yet that a like Union should be impractical for ten or a Dozen English Colonies, to whom it is more necessary, and must be more advantageous.[19]

The English also invited the Iroquois in southern New York and the Delaware of Pennsylvania to the Albany Congress. An important piece of the Albany Plan of Union proposed by Franklin was that the colonies treat the Indians fairly and consistently. Each colony had been negotiating with the tribes differently, often allowing land purchases and policies that took advantage of the Indians. The union Franklin proposed would have negotiated with Indian nations and regulated land expansions; it also would have coordinated the building of forts, the raising of armies, and the sharing of expenses for defense against renewed French pressures.

With the increased activity of the French in the Ohio Valley, it was possible that the Iroquois would rethink their loyalty to the English. The alliance between the Iroquois and the English had been

confederation in 1751. In a letter to a friend, Franklin maintained:

> It would be a very strange Thing, if six Nations of ignorant Savages should be capable of forming a Scheme for such a Union [the Iroquois League], and be able to execute it in such a Manner, as that it has [survived] for Ages, and

Adamant about the need for colonial union, Franklin graphically expressed his opinion with this drawing of a disjointed snake. Each segment is labeled with one name of a colony.

Tee Yee Heen Ho Ga Row, a chief of the Six Nations, displays a wampum belt.

sealed for years with wampum shells woven into symbolic belts exchanged between the two parties. The alliance was called the Covenant Chain, and the wampum shells were like signatures on a contract today.

At the Albany Congress, Iroquois leaders spoke openly of the old alliance but also about their fears. They were unhappy with many of the agreements with the English colonies, and they doubted that the English would protect them from the French. It was Indian land and villages, after all, that stood on the frontier closest to the new French forts. The Iroquois also complained that colonial decisions were made without consulting them, especially on issues related to native territory. Chief Hendrick of the Canajoharie Mohawks gave his assent to the pact in these candid terms:

> We do now solemnly renew and brighten the Covenant Chain with our Brethren on the Continent. The Governor of Virginia and the Governor of Canada are both quarreling about lands which belong to us . . . [and] the Governors of Virginia and Pennsylvania have made paths thro' our Country to Trade, and built houses [trading posts or forts] without acquainting us with it. They should first have asked our consent to build there, as was done when Oswego [New York] was built.[20]

When the Six Nations left Albany, they took with them thirty wagon loads of gifts from the English. The Albany Congress, however, did not succeed in winning full support from the Iroquois. Since maintaining a balance of power was still very important to the Iroquois, the Six Nations promised neutrality in case of war, nothing more. The English were left to gather their own forces against the French. As Thomas Pownall, an observer for the Board of Trade at the Albany Congress, noted:

> The Iroquois were conscious on one hand that their League and Alliance with the English might draw them into war on the French. On the other hand, they were really and in good earnest afraid of the French.
>
> And having no confidence or trust in any measures or promises we enter into, and finding that by our measures we are neither able nor willing to defend them, they were sensible that such a declaration of alliance with the English . . . must be the ruin of them. Their Resolution therefore was to observe a neutrality.[21]

Other discussions at the Albany Congress were also discouraging. There was no agreement for a strong, consistent approach by the colonies to the problems of land boundaries and Indian relations. Franklin's hopes for the Albany Plan of Union vanished. It would be ten more years before the colonies would be ready to unite.

Alarm in London

In London, the response to Washington's embarrassing defeat at Fort Necessity was outrage. England needed a swift and forceful retaliation to keep the French in their place—in Canada. Gen. Edward Braddock became commander-in-chief of the British forces in North America. He was assigned to lead nearly 2,000 British soldiers and colonial militia over the Appalachian Mountains to seize Fort

Gen. Edward Braddock commanded the British forces sent to seize Fort Duquesne from the French.

Duquesne. With forty-five years of military experience behind him, Braddock was confident that given enough men, he could easily take Fort Duquesne.

Braddock's expedition in the summer of 1755 was only part of a larger British plan to contain the French. In the spring of 1755, colonial governors met at Annapolis, Maryland. They outlined a four-part campaign against New France, even though war had not been declared. First, Governor Shirley of Massachusetts would lead a force to capture Fort Niagara, which protected the French trade link between Lake Ontario and Lake Erie. Then General Braddock would seize Fort Duquesne, later joining Shirley in triumph on Niagara's parade ground.

The third task set forth by the colonial strategists was to enhance the defense of the Champlain Valley by building forts to balance the French strongholds in place and under construction near the lake. Finally, a naval force would attack Fort Beausejour in Nova Scotia to remove the French from this area of Acadia. There was no declaration of war, and no European conflict. Yet the English anticipated that the year 1755 would record a series of decisive victories over the French empire in North America.

European Warfare

The British strategy was based on the well-established rule of warfare used in Europe. Grand confrontations on open, level fields were mapped out, to permit armies to face each other in an orderly manner. Battle etiquette was observed, and formal specific maneuvers were planned. Sea-

Wampum

Tiny shell beads woven into belts or other articles by Native Americans, wampum served as either money or a contract between two parties. In Realm of the Iroquois, *a volume of the Time-Life series on the American Indians, the role of wampum is explained.*

"The value [of wampum] to the Iroquois and neighboring tribes was more spiritual than monetary. Wampum, in reality, evoked the very founding of the Iroquois confederacy. According to legend, the [great] chief Hiawatha mourned the deaths of his wife and daughters. He met the prophet Deganawida, who consoled the grieving man with strings of white shells. (The word 'wampum' is derived from an Algonquian phrase meaning 'strings of white.') The two men, bonded in friendship, worked together to forge the league of tribes.

The Iroquois used the beads as memory aids to record tribal history and sacred pacts. They first traded for wampum with coastal tribes, who used conch and quahog shells. The white beads signify purity, and the purple ones stand for grief.

Wampum was . . . essential to diplomacy between the Iroquois and the Europeans. Before treaty talks, the Iroquois exchanged wampum as a sign of sincerity. When a pact was made, its terms were woven into a belt, and the agreement was sealed by a gift of wampum."

As a diplomatic gesture, a Native American leader presents a wampum belt to an English commander.

Terrorist attacks on isolated sites characterized French and Indian battles in North America.

soned colonial soldiers from King William's, Queen Anne's, and King George's wars, however, knew that in the New World battles could not be conducted in these traditional ways. There were few open fields. In addition, cannon and equipment had to be hauled long distances over rugged trails.

The enemy was not a well-disciplined, courtly army in colorful uniforms. Instead, the ranks of French forces had numbers of rough frontiersmen and bands of Hurons or Abenakis accustomed to wilderness fighting, as opposed to European-style combat. Terrorist attacks on isolated sites characterized French and Indian battles in North America. Winter battles also occurred in the harshest of weather, catching European troops unprepared.

Despite warnings by Benjamin Franklin, George Washington, and others, General Braddock was determined to approach Fort Duquesne on his own terms, in the standard European manner. He brushed off Washington's warning, announcing:

These savages may, indeed, be a formidable enemy to your raw American militia, but upon the King's regular and disciplined troops, sir, it is impossible they should make any impression.[22]

Braddock's Expedition

The crude wagon road made earlier by Washington's men to reach Fort Duquesne became the path for the next stage of the war. The simple camp at the road's origin on the east side of the mountains, now strengthened into Fort Cumberland, was the staging area for the expedition of 1755, much grander than Washington's. As Braddock's forces left Fort Cumberland in June to climb the Allegheny Mountains toward Fort Duquesne, they stretched for miles, marching four abreast. One hundred fifty Conestoga wagons of supplies and carriages of howitzers and field cannon completed the scene. Following Washington's original wagon trail, the troops labored to open up a proper road, slowing Braddock's progress to a crawl. As aide-de-camp to Braddock, George Washington advised the British general that it would be winter before the expedition reached Duquesne. By then, surely, the French would have reinforced the fort. Braddock agreed to lead an advance detachment of his best men, lightly equipped, to move swiftly over the mountains. Another aide-de-camp, Captain Orme, recorded the launch of the expedition:

July 18, 1755. At the Little Meadows a place about Twenty Miles from this, we found it unavoidable to alter our

Led by fife and drums, Braddock's disciplined troops march in tight ranks and orderly lines.

disposition of march, it being impossible to proceed with such a Train of Carriages. A detachment was therefore made of twelve hundred men, ten pieces of ordnance [artillery], ammunition, and provisions calculated for reducing the Fort [Duquesne] and our [survival].[23]

Washington's fears of reinforcements at Fort Duquesne were justified. Early in the summer, the fort had been lightly manned. By midsummer, however, reinforcements began arriving daily: the Potawatomi and Ottawa tribes from the western territories. Close to 700 Indians

gathered at the fort. The tribes were willing to fight on the side of the French to keep the British from increasing their strength in the Ohio Territory.

An Elaborate Ambush

As the British advanced in an orderly manner, the French and Indians fanned out through the terrain along the rough road, beginning an elaborate ambush named the Battle of the Wilderness. Braddock and his troops never had a chance: their gaudy uniforms were perfect targets, and their confinement on the narrow trail

Braddock's troops with their brightly colored uniforms were easy targets for the clever French and Indians.

Battle of the Wilderness

After the defeat and death of General Braddock, one of the English commander's aides-de-camp [assistants] wrote an account of the disastrous day in a letter to a friend. Captain Orme's manuscript was published by the American Antiquarian Society in 1909.

"July 18, 1755. The French with some Indians, the number of both unknown, had taken a very strong post about half a mile from the Banks of Monongahela; our advanced party, consisting of 300 men, began a very irregular & confused attack. They were ill sustained by 200 in their rear, and the whole fell back upon [the] main body, commanded by the General, whilst he was moving forward to their assistance. From this time all was anarchy, no order, no discipline, no subordination [obedience]. The General with the Officers endeavored to bring the men back to a sense of their duty, but all efforts were vain.

This Confusion lasted about two hours and a half, and then the whole ran off crying the devil take the hindmost. Our guns, ammunition, provisions and baggage remained in the hands of the enemy, and the General was with the greatest difficulty brought off being so much wounded as to be quite helpless. The General had five horses shot under him and at last received a shot through his lungs of which he died the 13th at night. . . . Washington alone escaped tho' no man deserved a wound better, his whole Behavior being extremely gallant."

made effective defense impossible. From behind trees, boulders, and hillocks, the French and Indians overwhelmed the advance troops with deadly musket fire.

As commander, Braddock did his best to rally the men into some manner of military discipline as they broke ranks, but he was soon mortally wounded himself, shot through the lungs. Only thirty or so French and Indian fatalities occurred in the Battle of the Wilderness. Of the approximately 1,400 English troops with Braddock, however, more than 900 were killed or wounded. Washington placed the dying general in an open cart to be taken from the line of battle, and Braddock admitted, "Had I been governed by your advice, we never should have come to this."[24]

During the battle, Braddock's field desk was captured and delivered to the commander of New France, Governor Vaudreuil, who was replacing Governor Duquesne. In the desk were several plans to seize Fort Niagara and attack Acadia's

English troops swiftly retreat from the Battle of the Wilderness with their fatally wounded commander in tow. After Braddock's defeat, the English colonies lost confidence in the British army's ability to defend them, and they turned to the American colonial leaders for protection.

Fort Beausejour. There were also notes about building a fort on Lake George to challenge French control of Lake Champlain. The new governor could not have been more pleased and immediately began work on his own plans to surprise and defeat the English.

With Braddock's defeat, the English colonies lost confidence in the king's army's ability to defend them. Ben Franklin spoke for many when he observed: "This whole Transaction [Braddock's defeat] gave us Americans the first Suspicion that our exalted Ideas of the Prowess of British Regulars had not been well founded."[25] In the next few years, the English colonies depended increasingly on proven American colonial leaders and their own initiative to protect themselves from French and Indian raids and expansion.

5 The Champlain Valley Crucible: 1755-1756

The four-part English campaign to defeat the French began to dissolve the day General Braddock lost the Battle of the Wilderness. Then Governor Shirley of Massachusetts, upon discovering that France had reinforced Fort Niagara, abandoned the goal of capturing it. There was some satisfaction, however, in the seizure of small Fort Beausejour in Acadia. By late 1755, only one piece remained of the great British scheme to humble France: the defense of the crucial Champlain Valley in Iroquois country, near the heart of the English colonies. This important assignment was given to colonial leader William Johnson.

William Johnson

Soon after opening a small trading post on the Mohawk River in 1738, William Johnson had become the most successful trader in the Mohawk region. Johnson was unique in that he developed a great appreciation for the Iroquois nations, eventually marrying a Canajoharie Mohawk woman, Molly Brant. Johnson acquired hundreds of acres of land from the Indians in the area, primarily around present Johnstown, in central New York. He built a

great house—Johnson Hall—on his land. Named superintendent of Indian affairs in the northern colonies in 1755, Johnson was assigned to protect the Champlain Valley if the French resumed their raids on the frontier. Gathering together Iroquois warriors, mostly Mohawk, and assorted

Colonial leader William Johnson joined with Iroquois warriors to confront French advances in the Champlain Valley.

colonial militia, Johnson prepared to confront the French advance. Just as New France was building new forts in the Ohio Valley, it was also strengthening the French presence in the Champlain Valley.

After Braddock's defeat, the French immediately began to pressure the Iroquois nations, hoping to break their alliance with the English. Governor Vaudreuil sent strong words to the Senecas and Cayugas, the two Iroquois tribes who occasionally fought on the side of the French:

> Should any of the [Iroquois] be found next spring among the English, I will let loose all our Upper and [Canadian Indian] Nations on them; cause their villages to be laid waste and never pardon them.[26]

Vaudreuil's threat had little effect, however, on the one man who had more influence on relations between the English and the Iroquois than anyone else, William Johnson. The English colonial leader had learned to speak the Mohawk language and spent time in their camps. He was given a Mohawk name: Warraghiyagey, "man who understands great things." Johnson's influence on the Iroquois is made clear in comments he wrote to a friend in 1750 about a Cayuga chief:

> Until last Summer [he] was intirely in the French Interest . . . and the reason he gave me was, that the French he thought were a more warlike people than we, and being the Head Warrior of the five Nations Himself, Said he had a veneration for all those of his own dis-

At right, William Johnson meets with a Native American leader in this somewhat fanciful illustration. Johnson developed favorable relations with the Iroquois and easily gained their support. Governor Vaudreuil of New France (left) could do little to prevent the Iroquois tribes from joining the British effort against the French.

William Johnson, Manager of Indian Affairs

After the Albany Congress of 1754, the colonies petitioned the king of England to put William Johnson in charge of Indian affairs. The request appears in Empire of Fortune *by Francis Jennings.*

"Colonel Johnson should be appointed Colonel over the Six [Iroquois] Nations. . . . The reasons of our taking the liberty to recommend this Gentleman to Your Majesty are the representations which have been made to us of the great service he did during [King George's War]. [He] preserved the friendship of the Indians and engaged them to take up the hatchet against the French. [He has] connexions he has formed by living amongst them, and habituating himself to their manners and customs. The publick testimony [of the Iroquois] they have given at the last meeting of their friendship for, and confidence in, him. Above all the request they make [is] that the sole management of their affairs may be intrusted to him."

position. Besides, they [the French] always used him better by far than our own People [the British], until such time as he got acquainted with me, whence commenced his friendship with us, which I have been at a great deal of pains and Expence to Cultivate.[27]

English Forts in the Champlain Valley

Under the four-part campaign, Johnson's task was to erect English forts to balance the two French forts on Lake Champlain. Fort St. Frederic had been built at Crown Point in 1731, but Fort Carillon, which was slowly rising at Ticonderoga, would put the French in a much stronger position on the lake. When the fort at Ticonderoga was completed, the French would be able to guard the little channel connecting Lakes George and Champlain. The second crucial connector in the water route between the St. Lawrence and the Hudson River was the Great Carrying Place, an overland trail between Lake George and the Hudson River. William Johnson rushed to raise a small fort, Fort Edward, at the headwaters of the Hudson River, at the southern tip of Lake George, the other end of the connector. With these two forts in place, the English felt more secure.

The battle for the forts in the Champlain Valley required tactics different from those used in the formal siege of Louisbourg. Hit-and-run wilderness combat depended for success on competence in reading the weather and terrain. Colonial scouts, or rangers, accompanied every British army in the New World. These

A view of Lake George shows piles of ammunition that lie ready to repel French invaders. The English acted to prevent the French from controlling the overland trail connecting Lake George and the Hudson River.

rangers brought news of enemy movements and guided British troops through the wilderness. Robert Rogers of New Hampshire commanded a tough force of frontiersmen who became famous as "Rogers' Rangers." They later fought with William Johnson's troops at the Battle of Lake George, gaining the respect of English military professionals and Native American warriors alike. More like Indians than British regulars, the rangers fought in all kinds of terrain, in the worst of seasons, and from canoes and snowshoes as well as on foot.

To report on activity in the French forts, English colonial scouts like Rogers' Rangers were sent out regularly to spy on enemy installations. The details they brought to Johnson about construction progress and troop strength were very valuable. Rogers recorded in his journal:

Tough and rugged frontiersmen called Rogers' Rangers wage battle against the French on Lake George.

November 12, 1755: Proceeded with a party of ten men, upon a scout, to ascertain the enemy's strength and condition at Ticonderoga, and on the 14th, arrived in sight of the Fort. The enemy had erected three new barracks and four store houses in the Fort, between which and the water, they had eighty batteaux [flat-bottomed rowboats] hauled up on the beach. They had fifty tents near the Fort, and appeared to be very busily employed in strengthening their works. Having attained our object, we reached camp on the 19th.

December 19, 1755: After a month's repose, I embarked with two men, once more, to reconnoitre [spy on] the French at Ticonderoga. On our way a fire was discovered upon an Island near the Fort, which we supposed to have been kindled by the enemy. This obliged us to lie by, and act like fishermen, to deceive them, until night came on, when we gained the west shore 15 miles north of our camp. Concealing our boat we pursued our march by land on the 20th and on the 21st at noon, reached the Fort. The enemy were still engaged in their works, and had mounted four pieces of cannon on the south east bastion. . . . They mustered about 500 men. . . . On the 24th we returned to Fort William Henry, a fortress erected this year at the south end of Lake George. . . . [William] Johnson and the [New England] Commissioners judge it most prudent to leave one company of woodsmen, or Rangers under my command, to make excursions to the enemy's forts during the winter; and we remained with the Garrison.[28]

The Battle of Lake George

French activity at Crown Point and Ticonderoga intensified after General Braddock's defeat. Governor Vaudreuil of New

---

Rogers' Rangers Become a Special Unit

In 1756, Robert Rogers was commissioned to create and command a special unit of scouts, or rangers. Rogers reported the event in his journal, which was published in Reminiscences of the French War.

"March 1756: On the 23d the General [commander in chief Shirley] gave me a friendly reception, and the next day a commission to recruit an independent corps of Rangers. It was ordered that the Corps should consist of sixty privates. . . . None were to be enlisted [unless they were] accustomed to travelling, and hunting, and in whose courage and fidelity the most implicit confidence could be placed. They were moreover to be subject to military discipline, and the articles of war. The rendezvous was appointed at Albany, whence to proceed in whale boats to Lake George, and [here Rogers quotes his orders] 'from time to time, to use their best endeavours to distress the French and their allies, by sacking, burning, and destroying their houses, barns, barracks, canoes, batteaux, &c. and by killing their cattle of every kind; and at all times to endeavour to waylay, attack, and destroy their convoys of provision, by land and water, in any part of the country, where they could be found.'"

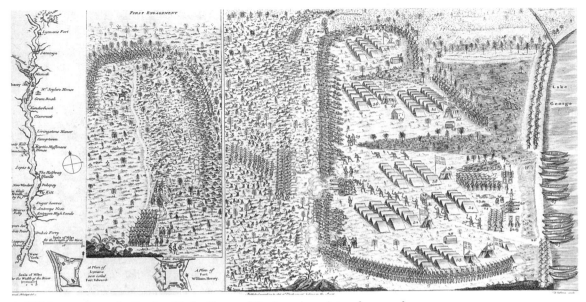

*A 1756 map shows the Battle of Lake George. His stunning victory here made
Johnson a hero to the English and the colonists.*

France was eager to move his troops and
take advantage of the surprise gift that
had fallen into his hands: the British master plan from General Braddock's field
desk. Vaudreuil saw the possibility of turn-
ing the British plan upside down if he
could move quickly enough.

Commanding the reinforcements sent
to Crown Point was Baron Dieskau, second to Vaudreuil himself. Dieskau hoped
to ambush the untrained Yankee farmers
and Mohawk allies that William Johnson
had assembled for an attack on Crown
Point. If successful, Dieskau would hand
them the kind of devastating defeat that
had befallen General Braddock.

Johnson's encampment on the banks
of Lake George was suddenly attacked by
Dieskau's French regulars and their
Caughnawaga Mohawk allies. Oddly
enough, Dieskau made the same mistake
Braddock had made. He insisted on con-
fining his white-uniformed French troops

to tight ranks and orderly lines. Moreover,
he lost much of his strength when Johnson and his Mohawk allies secretly com-
municated to Dieskau's Caughnawaga
Mohawks. Johnson's Mohawks persuaded
the French Mohawks not to join the attack
on their English Mohawk brothers. The
Caughnawaga Mohawks refused to advance, and the British fought the Battle of
Lake George to a standstill, capturing
Baron Dieskau in the process.

Even though Johnson had not
achieved his goal of seizing the fort at
Crown Point, his defense against the
French surprise attack made him a hero in
English and colonial eyes. The British Par-
liament credited him with halting the
French advance up the Champlain Valley.

For the English, the Battle of Lake
George took some of the sting out of the
shame of the Battle of the Wilderness.
Vaudreuil was humiliated by the capture
of his second in command and furious at

the loss of the advantage he had gained from Braddock's papers. By 1756, France and England had fought major battles in the New World once more, and each had experienced defeat. These battles forced the British and French empires back into war. By May 1756, Great Britain had declared war on France. Thus began the French and Indian War in North America and the Seven Years' War in Europe.

Titus King, A Captive Colonial Soldier

Titus King of Northampton, Massachusetts, captured by Indians in 1755, described his experiences in a journal. He also recorded the French reaction to Braddock's defeat. Narrative of Titus King of Northampton *retains King's odd spelling and loose punctuation. It may be easier to understand if it is read out loud.*

"July 24, 1755: I had not been there [at the Canadian village of St. Francis] more than an houre before the French Prest that had the Care of the Indians Came to See me he asked what Religon I was . . . he asked me [if] I was Catlotlick I told him I Profast to be but not a Roman he told ye god had Done great things for me in Leting the Indians bring me there where there was a good Religon & that now I had oppertunity to be Saved I told him I Called Captivity a Sore Judgment of god but yet I hoped it would be for the best the French was then Very much Rage with Braddox Defeet which was about this time which I Shall menshon here & Sume outher Victorys in the two or 3 following years which greatly Prompt the French [and] mad them insult the poor Prisoners the more.

In the year 1755 Braddock Had his Defeet himself Slane and his army Brok Slain & Scattered this Occasioned Great joy amongst the French: In the yr 1756 The French army went out against Oswego & Took it brought 1500 Presiners about a 100 of Which Died in Canada The following winter about 700 French Went Down to Fort William henry & burnt ye Vesels: & about 200 battwos [batteaux]

When Fort William Henry was taken the English had the Small Pox amongst them & So brought it a way with them Sume of them Died haveing no Care taken of them in there Sorfull State of Captivety . . . it was Said yet they gave it to these Wild Indians as they are Calld many of which Died the Small Pox amoungst them is more Fatal than a army of men"

English, French, and Mohawks fight fiercely at the Battle of Lake George (left). After Baron Dieskau's humiliating defeat in the battle, France sent Louis Joseph, Marquis de Montcalm (below), to command the French troops.

After Braddock's defeat and Dieskau's capture, both empires dispatched new military commanders to North America. John Campbell, earl of Loudoun, was sent by England, and Louis Joseph, Marquis de Montcalm, arrived in Quebec from France. Montcalm was clearly the superior general. His many years of experience fighting for France in Europe had made him a clever tactician. He was intense, decisive, and accustomed to exercising absolute authority. Competent and forceful, Loudoun was often slowed down by his concern for detail.

Montcalm's first move upon arriving in Canada was to inspect the construction

of Fort Carillon at Ticonderoga. Satisfied that the work was progressing, he wasted no time in mobilizing against the English Fort Oswego on Lake Ontario. The French had long viewed the presence of Fort Oswego as a major irritant: it was the only English fort interrupting the string of French forts along the Great Lakes. In 1727 Oswego's "fortified stone house" had been built on the trading post site, garrisoned by a small English force.

Fort Oswego

At the Annapolis conference with Braddock in 1754, the representatives of the English colonies had emphasized the danger to Fort Oswego if French power expanded in the region. Thus work to strengthen the old post was authorized immediately. By 1755, some reinforcements had arrived, and shipwrights had been sent to construct several small warships for Lake Ontario. Two small bastions were begun on either side of the heights overlooking Oswego. Located at the extreme end of the British supply line, however, Oswego remained lightly defended and thinly provisioned. Montcalm's troops easily took the fort by firing on it with Braddock's own cannon, seized after the Battle of the Wilderness. When the fort surrendered, thirty English soldiers captured inside were killed, continuing the pattern of terror sponsored by the French.

Montcalm immediately doubled back to the Champlain Valley to attack Fort William Henry, the new English post on Lake George. By the summer of 1757, the log fort was under heavy siege. Smallpox raged inside the compound, and within days the commander was forced to surrender. William Johnson had made a dramatic last-minute attempt to come to the aid of the fort, but his plea was rejected by General Webb, commander at Fort Edward. A French aide-de-camp recorded the exchange between Johnson and Webb:

I learned from the Sault St. Louis Indians, who keep up contact with their Mohawk brothers, of a fine scene that happened during the last campaign. While we were besieging Fort William Henry, Johnson, Dieskau's conqueror, arrived at Fort Edward at the head of 800 provincials, Mohawks, and Moraigans [Mohegans], a sort of bastard tribe; [Johnson was] all in war paint like his troop, tomahawk at his side, halberd [a long pole with a spearlike weapon mounted on the top] in hand. He proposed to General Webb to march at once on the French lines. Webb said he would not, that he did not wish to expose himself to a complete defeat in woods already red with English blood. Johnson replied that these same shores of Lake George would be as fatal to Montcalm as they had been to Dieskau, that French bones would cover this battlefield where, he swore by his halberd and tomahawk, he would conquer or die. General Webb was not moved. Johnson then . . . tore off one of his leggings and hurled it at Webb's feet. "You won't do it?" said he. "No." Tore off the other legging. "You won't?" Hurled a garter. "You won't?" Hurled his shirt, tomahawk, and halberd down, and galloped off with his troop who had imitated his actions entirely. Where is Homer [poet-storyteller of the Trojan Wars of ancient Greece] to paint such scenes more Greek than Greek?[29]

James Fenimore Cooper

Novelist James Fenimore Cooper shaped public opinion about the era of the French and Indian War. His books were about Indians noble and wicked and frontier heroes. Cooper's 1840 book The Pathfinder *has a hero reminiscent of one of Rogers' Rangers.*

" 'Fear nothing, young woman,' said the hunter, for such his attire would indicate him to be. 'You have met Christian men in the wilderness, and such as know how to treat all kindly who are disposed to peace and justice. I am a man well known in these parts, and perhaps one of my names may have reached your ears. By the Frenchers and the redskins on the other side of the Big Lakes I am called La Longue Carabine [Long Rifle]; by the Mohicans, a just-minded and upright tribe, what is left of them, Hawk Eye; while the troops and rangers along this side of the water call me Pathfinder, inasmuch as I have never been known to miss one end of the trail, when there was a Mingo [an enemy Indian], or a friend who stood in need of me, at the other.' "

An illustration from James Fenimore Cooper's The Pathfinder *depicts the story's noble hero ready to confront the enemy.*

Montcalm negotiated surrender terms with the commander of Fort William Henry, but the usual formal European surrender terms were not enforced by the French officers. Instead of permitting an orderly and safe evacuation of the fort, Montcalm allowed a massacre of wounded and sick English soldiers and civilians by the Indian allies of the French. This act, following the similar slaughter at Fort Oswego, further horrified and enraged the English colonies.

The Second Louisbourg Expedition

While Montcalm was completing his campaign to reclaim the New York region for New France, the earl of Loudoun was ordered by London to attack Louisbourg. British leaders were convinced that Loudoun's professional troops could easily repeat the extraordinary victory of William Pepperell's rustic colonials in 1745. The colonies refused to unite behind Loudoun, however. Delay after delay prevented the troops from moving out of Halifax, Nova Scotia, to take Louisbourg, which was not far up the coast. A colonial soldier recorded his perspective:

> As if delay had been an essential part of their instructions, near a month was consumed at Halifax in exercising the troops. . . . These steps were condemned by some as "keeping the courage of his Majesty's soldiers at bay and expending the nation's wealth in making sham fights and planting cabbages when they ought to have been fighting the enemies of their king and country."[30]

Before Loudoun could get underway, the French fleet arrived at Louisbourg to reinforce it. Loudoun called off his expedition, and the last hope that the British navy could blockade the French fleet in Louisbourg harbor was abandoned when a fierce storm destroyed much of the British fleet.

The impact of the year's disappointments was keenly felt in the English colonies as well as in London. In 1756 the Protestant theologian Jonathan Edwards wrote to a chaplain friend stationed with a Massachusetts regiment on Lake George:

> God indeed is remarkably frowning upon us everywhere; our enemies get up above us very high, and we are brought down very low: They are the Head, and we are the Tail. God is making us, with all our superiority in numbers, to become the Object of our Enemies almost continual Triumphs and Insults. . . . And in Europe things don't go much better. . . . Minorca was surrendered to the French on the 29 Day of last June; principally through the wretched Cowardice or Treachery of Admiral Bying. This with the taking of Oswego . . . will tend mightily to animate and encourage the French Nation . . . and weaken and dishearten the English, and make 'em contemptible in the Eyes of the Nations of Europe. . . . What will become of us God only knows.[31]

Thus ended the great ambitions of the British empire in 1756 and 1757. With Fort Oswego reduced to ashes and Fort William Henry destroyed, the British colonial frontier had been forced back to Albany as, one by one, the outlying British forts in New York gave way before the French. Braddock's defeat had effectively ended English expansion across the Appalachian Mountains. The English colonies were squeezed back between the mountains and the coast, exactly as the French had hoped they would be. The only question that remained was whether New France could keep her frontier "necklace" of forts around the English colonies intact.

Chapter

6 Master Plan for Victory

After the series of defeats suffered in 1755 and 1756, the British government was in an uproar. The worldwide war it had undertaken was adrift and out of control. Cabinets rose and fell swiftly as the empire lurched from crisis to crisis. By mid-1757, however, Prime Minister William Pitt was finally able to form a united government in London. He won the cooperation of the American colonies and began the process of reversing British fortunes.

William Pitt understood that enormous commitments would be necessary to bring success to British efforts around the world. He made plans to spend huge sums and spare no expense to support renewed military campaigns in North America. Pitt recognized the value of the colonial militia and placed great emphasis on keeping them well supplied. In his letter to the colonial assemblies, Pitt was specific about the support he promised:

William Pitt launched a grand strategy to end France's control in the New World.

> The King [George II] is further pleased to furnish all the [colonial] Men . . . with Arms, Ammunition, and Tents, as well as to order Provisions to be issued to the same, by His Majesty's Commissaries, in the same Proportion and Manner as is done to the rest of the King's Forces:
>
> A sufficient Train of Artillery will also be provided, at His Majesty's Ex-

pense, for the Operations of the Campaign. . . . The Whole, therefore, that His Majesty expects and requires from the several Provinces, is the Levying, Cloathing, and Pay of the Men;

And, on these Heads also, that no Encouragement may be wanting to this great and salutary Attempt, The King is farther most Graciously pleased to permit me to acquaint You,

French Troops at Ticonderoga

Robert Rogers and his Rangers often captured French soldiers caught off guard outside their forts, or French farmers living in the Champlain Valley. For example, a French soldier and his family provided this valuable information to the British just before Montcalm's attack on Fort William Henry. The account is recorded in Reminiscences of the French War.

"The Frenchman stated . . . he had been in Canada 15 years, in the Colonies' service six, and two years at Crown Point; that [Crown] Point was garrisoned by only 300 men, and those mostly inhabitants of the villages adjacent; that 4000 men occupied Ticonderoga . . . 1500 of which were regular troops, who had plenty of all kinds of provisions and stores;—that he never was at [Ticonderoga], or the advanced guard; but heard there were only 15 men at the latter;

that 600 Indians were at [Ticonderoga], and 600 more expected; that 1200 had reached Quebec on their way to [Ticonderoga]; that Ticonderoga was well supplied with cannon, mortars, shells, shot &c; that garrison expected a reinforcement in two or three days, having sent boats to Montreal to bring troops;

that he had heard by letter that [British Fort] Oswego had fallen into the hands of the French, but it was not yet confirmed; that they kept 150 batteaux on the Lake [Ontario], 35 of which went between Montreal and [Ticonderoga];

that vessels had arrived at Quebec with provisions and military stores."

that strong Recommendations will be made to Parliament in their Session next Year, to grant a proper Compensation for such Expences as above.[32]

The grand strategy for victory in the New World was no surprise. It featured some of the same plans the British had tried in earlier wars against the French. The difference was that William Pitt committed great sums of money and large numbers of troops to the war effort. Massive attacks would target Louisbourg, Fort Carillon at Ticonderoga on Lake Champlain, and Fort Duquesne in the Ohio country. After taking Louisbourg, an English fleet would sail up the St. Lawrence. At the same time, English troops would capture Ticonderoga and march up the Champlain Valley to meet the fleet at Quebec. At Quebec, a decisive British victory over New France would finally settle the question of control of the New World.

Moves against Louisbourg began as soon as Pitt came to power in London. In June 1757 the English fleet finally gained

James Wolfe discusses his battle plans with Pitt before departing for Louisbourg.

a small landing area near the fortress after days of heavy seas and dense fog. The jagged, rocky coast afforded few landing sites, and James Wolfe, a young British officer, followed Pepperell's footsteps to the beachhead the colonists had successfully stormed in 1745. When Wolfe's whaleboats landed, however, the men were stunned by a French ambush. Inching forward, the soaked British redcoats eventually forced the ambush party slowly back toward the walls of Louisbourg.

The sheltered harbor at Louisbourg was defended by 400 cannon. Some were placed at the Royal Battery inside the harbor, and the remainder were at the Island Battery facing the fortress across a narrow channel. Within the citadel, or fortress, and the town were 4,000 French troops, hundreds of Abenakis, and more than 2,000 sailors. Bearing down on Louisbourg were more than 14,000 British colonials, regular soldiers, and sailors. When Wolfe made his landing, his men hauled British cannon closer and closer to the fortress walls. At the same time, the navy returned the fire of the cannon of the Island Battery guarding the harbor.

Heavy bombardment of the fortress followed. The French commander at Louisbourg, Ducour, wanted to hold out until the arrival of winter weather, which would have prevented the British from moving up the St. Lawrence against Quebec. Seven weeks later, however, the town and fort were reduced to flaming rubble, and French ships burned in the harbor. Ducour agreed to surrender. At noon on July 27, 1758, English troops under the command of Gen. Jeffrey Amherst marched into Louisbourg. The captured French flag was sent to London to hang in St. Paul's Cathedral, and General Amherst wrote this message to William Pitt: "If I can go to Quebeck, I will."[33]

Disaster at Ticonderoga

While the battle for Louisbourg was taking place, British and colonial troops gathered for an attack on Fort Carillon at Ticonderoga. Besides Rogers' Rangers and twelve colonial regiments, Gen. James Abercromby had seven regiments of British regulars, about 12,000 in all. The British army was floated up Lake George in a six-mile-long colorful parade of batteaux, fishing dories, and dozens of flatboats carrying artillery to the landing site where Lake George connects with Champlain.

General Montcalm led only 3,000 French and Indian troops within the new star-shaped fort at Ticonderoga, on Lake Champlain. Fearing a lengthy siege, which he knew he could not survive, Montcalm moved quickly to set up a zigzag defense line across the approach to the fort.

The great numerical superiority of the British army should have guaranteed victory. Abercromby was overly cautious, however, allowing Montcalm time to strengthen his forward defense line. When the battle finally commenced in the heat of the day, the British troops were ordered ahead in the classic European tradition of warfare. Rank upon rank, they marched into enemy fire and were mowed down by the French, firing from behind their zigzag line.

An illustration published in 1762 depicts the ruinous remains of Louisbourg after English forces besieged the city in 1758.

Rogers' Rangers, hidden in the woods outside the fort, saved the ragged retreat of the British. The Rangers protected the fleeing English troops by firing steadily into the French line. Nearly 2,000 British troops were killed or wounded, while the French lost fewer than 400. Both armies were exhausted by the intense battle. If Montcalm had pushed his troops to pur-sue the British, however, he might have captured the entire army and given the French a major victory. Instead, he pro-tected his position near the fort. Robert Rogers described the defeat at Ticondero-ga in a matter-of-fact report in his journal:

July 6. After a fatiguing march of one hour, I reached [the] place which I was ordered and posted my men to

Destruction of Louisbourg

The fort of Louisbourg was named a National Historic Site by the Canadian government in 1940, and the reconstruction of the fort itself began in 1961. A great deal of archaeological and historical research continues at the site. A catalog by Edward Larrabee in the Canadian Historic Sites series, "Archaeological Research at the Fortress of Louisbourg, 1961-1965," summarizes what happened to the fort after it fell to the British in 1758.

"The year after the Treaty of Aix-la-Chapelle, 1748, [Cape Breton Island] was returned to the French, who strengthened the fortifications of Louisbourg and stood a second siege in the summer of 1758. General Amherst was in charge of British forces, but the systematic and energetic attack was under the direct command of Gen-eral Wolfe. Again the same weak points in the fortifica-tions were battered [as in 1745]. Again the French were caught short of supplies at the end of the winter, and the fortress surrendered.

The main British base at Halifax had an excellent harbour and so the British had little need of Louis-bourg. Fearing that at the forthcoming peace negotia-tions Louisbourg might again be returned to the French, the British systematically destroyed the fortifica-tions. The French occupants had already been sent back to France, and the town was in a ruinous condition as a result of the siege.

A small British garrison remained until 1768, when it was withdrawn to New England. The inhabitants of the town comprised a few ex-soldiers and settlers, chiefly from Ireland. The 19th-century occupation of the site consisted of a few families who fished and who farmed the now va-cant space within the shattered walls, or grazed sheep on all that remained of the French town and its defenses."

the best advantage; being within a quarter of a mile of where the Marquis de Montcalm, was posted with 1,500 men, as my scouts ascertained. . . .

July 7. . . . The whole army passed the night under arms. At sunrise on the 8th, Sir William Johnson arrived with 440 Indians. . . . At 7 o'clock, the Rangers were ordered to march . . . soon after, two provincial Regiments, formed in my rear, at 200 yards distance. While the army was thus forming, a scattering fire was kept up between our flying parties and those of the enemy. At half past ten, the greater part of the army being drawn up, a sharp fire commenced. . . .

We toiled with repeated attacks for four hours, being greatly embarrassed [inconvenienced] by trees felled by the enemy, when the General [Abercromby] ordered a retreat, and directed the Rangers to bring up the rear, which they did in the dusk of the evening.[34]

The bells ringing in London over the victory at Louisbourg were silenced when discouraging news finally crossed the Atlantic: the Ticonderoga expedition had failed.

Fort Frontenac

The shameful defeat of Abercromby's troops at Ticonderoga overshadowed a significant victory by Col. John Bradstreet shortly after the disaster at Lake Champlain. Although born an Acadian, Bradstreet was loyal to the British, and he begged Abercromby for permission to strike deep into enemy territory, attacking Fort Frontenac on Lake Erie. Bradstreet had been with Pepperell when Louisbourg was captured in 1745, and he had a reputation for audacity and effectiveness. In August 1758 Bradstreet and about 3,000 colonial troops departed from the ruins of Fort Oswego for a secret assault on the lightly defended Frontenac. The fort's commander surrendered to Bradstreet in two days, with no loss of life on either side.

The capture of Fort Frontenac, which effectively cut off French contact with Forts Niagara and Duquesne, was of enormous importance. This action also severed the French link with Lake Ontario. Bradstreet seized the French ships that patrolled the lakes, loaded them with the cannon and supplies that the defenders had abandoned, and burned the fort. Fort Frontenac's treasure of supplies was then delivered by water to the site of Fort Oswego. From there Bradstreet could maintain connection with British supply lines.

A military historian later wrote of the extraordinary stockpile seized by Bradstreet at the fort:

Through the wide-open gates of Fort Frontenac, Lieutenant Colonel John Bradstreet walked into a treasure trove. The warehouses were filled with the concentration of materiel needed to see the western forts through the coming winter. Seventy-six cannon, mounted and unmounted, were listed by the blue-coated British gunners making their check lists of the ordnance stores. Some of these pieces belonged to the seven unrigged vessels in the builder's yard. Bradstreet had himself rowed out to the two full-rigged vessels lying at anchor. He had last seen them two summers before, flying British colors at Oswego.

Now British colors flew again, [and] one of the vessels was fully laden with a rich cargo of stinking peltry, 30,000 [pounds sterling] of beautiful furs.

As the British sailed away, they estimated that they had destroyed 800,000 [in pounds sterling] of French materiel and stores. They had, of course, done more: they had wrecked the fort and destroyed the French shipping, cutting the lines to the source of the Great Lakes. On the Ohio, post commanders would not be able to feed their men nor hold their Indians with gifts and bounty.[35]

In strategic importance, Frontenac was perhaps even more critical than the fort at Ticonderoga. Its destruction was not fully appreciated nor greeted with cheers in London, but Governor Vaudreuil of New France knew that the protective French necklace of forts had been seriously damaged.

Quakers Encourage Negotiations

An important third piece of William Pitt's strategy to win the war against France included taking Fort Duquesne from the French. To approach Duquesne, troops needed to march through Indian territory in western Pennsylvania. French pressure on the western tribes had resulted in attacks and harassment on Pennsylvania settlers, primarily by the Delawares. There were numerous Pennsylvanians advocating more military force to end the attacks, but a core of Quakers encouraged peaceful negotiation between both sides.

Gen. John Forbes, commander of the English colonial troops, discovered valuable support among the Pennsylvania Quakers working toward a peaceful settlement. Quaker Israel Pemberton, Moravian Christian Frederic Post, and the Quaker Friendly Society served as intermediaries between the tribes and the English officers. Post rode on countless journeys of negotiation to work out agreements with the Delaware, Seneca, and Cayuga peoples. The British were persuaded that peace with the tribes was necessary to prevent the Indians from joining the French in the region. As Israel Pemberton wrote:

In his efforts against the French and Fort Duquesne, Gen. John Forbes sought strong alliances with the Indians to keep them from siding with the French.

Luke Gridley's Diary

Luke Gridley was a captain based at Fort Edward in the Champlain Valley in 1757. Gridley's diary is printed with the author's original spelling and punctuation. It may be easier to understand if the material is read out loud. Luke Gridley's Diary of 1757 *was published by the Acorn Club of Hartford, Connecticut, in 1906.*

"June Day 16th Brought into fort Edward a frinch man which told us: fore men & 5 scalps was Carryed to ticonderoge the 12 of June; that they Lost 7 of thare men the 10 of June wen these were Killd & taken: Allso that thare was two Battalyens of Regelar troops at Ticonderoge & a Large army at Crowne Pinte

Day 23th Thursday we Comeing jest of from Dewty 100 of our men was Calld away to mend highways Between the forts a Regler was whipd 100 Lashes for hollowing & scaring the Ennemy when Gennerel Limon had them partly ambusht

Day 24th three men whipt

July Day 2th six man taken with small pox: 2 men whipt for Being Drunk

Day 4th galard list Ranger 2 men Died with Camp Destemper 1 Limons man the other of Boston sorses: the number of men that have ye small pox In ye horseptell about 50 Rod from the fort Is 101:

Day 7th Johnathan Tilor John Willson: Charls Galard Left our tent for Rangers thare Compenney was Sursposed to Be verry good But thare Room much Better

Day 10th which was the sabath 18 of Cap Rogers men killed & taken near Crown pint one frinch prisner"

If General Forbes succeeds, it must be attributed rather to the drawing off of the Indians by our pacific Negotiations than anything else . . . [otherwise] I have reason to conclude he would not have ventur'd this Year to Ft. duQuesne.[36]

A peace treaty signed at Easton, Pennsylvania, in October 1758 between the Quakers, the Pennsylvania government, and Teedyuscung, the Delaware chief, ended the harassment raids on the colony's frontier settlers. The Easton treaty established a boundary line between colonial Pennsylvanian settlements and specified tribal territory. It was this boundary line that the British later honored, to prevent wars between Native Americans and colonial settlers. No English settlements were to be permitted past this line. The peace message sent to

Washington and his troops raise the British flag at Fort Duquesne after finding the fort burned and abandoned by the French.

the tribes after the Easton meeting was accompanied by gifts of wampum belts:

> Brethren on the Ohio: If you take the Belts we just now gave you, in which all here join, English and Indians, as we don't doubt you will, then by this Belt, I make a Road for you. We will invite you to come to Philadelphia to your first Old Council Fire, which was kindled when we first saw one another, which fire we will kindle up again and remove all disputes, and renew the Old and first Treaties of Friendship; . . . We desire all Tribes and Nations of Indians who are in Alliance with you may come.[37]

The Easton treaty also helped to persuade the Ohio Valley Indians to withdraw their support of Fort Duquesne. With the fall of Fort Frontenac, Duquesne was now cut off from French supplies and reinforcements. The fort was less and less defensible. As soon as the Easton treaty was signed, Forbes was ready to move against Duquesne, with an army that included George Washington and his Virginia regiments. Instead of using the rough and unlucky road traveled by General Braddock to Fort Duquesne, Forbes insisted on building a new wilderness cartway through Pennsylvania. The army of colonials inched forward in November 1758, only to find Fort Duquesne burned and abandoned by the French. The French commander, facing the prospect of a humiliating defeat, had chosen instead a smoldering signal of defiance and a safe retreat.

Pittsburgh

General Forbes celebrated the abandonment of the site of Fort Duquesne by the French, even though he was deprived of a noble military victory that would have been saluted in London. Standing amidst the fort's ruins, he renamed the site Pittsburgh in honor of William Pitt. A British garrison held the position through the long winter and began building Fort Pitt in the spring. A member of Forbes's escort party recorded the success of the Forbes expedition to Fort Duquesne in this way, failing to include the role played by the Quakers:

> After God, the success of this Expedition is intirely due to the General [Forbes], who by bringing about the Treaty of Easton, has struck the blow which has knocked the French in the head. The Effects of that Treaty secured all his posts and gave nothing to chance. [Forbes did] not yield to the urging instances for taking Braddock's Road, which would have been our destruction.[38]

George Washington had a somewhat different view of the successful march on Duquesne:

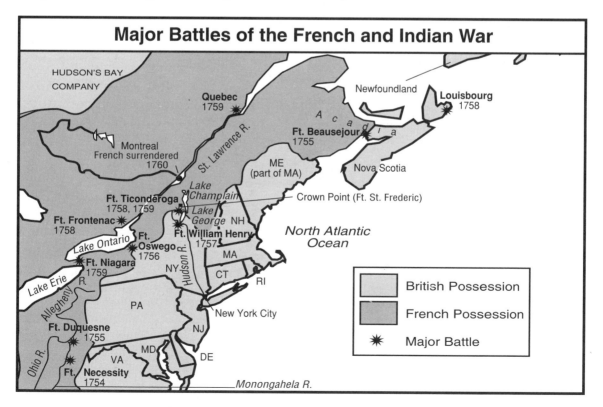

Major Battles of the French and Indian War

HUDSON'S BAY COMPANY

Quebec 1759

Newfoundland

Louisbourg 1758

Montreal French surrendered 1760

Acadia

Ft. Beausejour 1755

ME (part of MA)

St. Lawrence R.

Nova Scotia

Ft. Ticonderoga 1758, 1759

Lake Champlain

Crown Point (Ft. St. Frederic)

Ft. Frontenac 1758

Lake George NH

Lake Ontario

Ft. Oswego 1756

Ft. William Henry 1757

North Atlantic Ocean

Ft. Niagara 1759

Lake Erie

Allegheny R.

Hudson R.

MA

CT

RI

NY

PA

New York City

NJ

Ft. Duquesne 1755

Ohio R.

MD

DE

VA

Ft. Necessity 1754

Monongahela R.

	British Possession
	French Possession
✳	Major Battle

The possession of this fort has been a matter of great surprise to the whole army, and we cannot attribute it to more probable causes than those of weakness [at the fort], want of provisions, and desertion of their Indians.[39]

John Forbes himself wrote to William Pitt the following words:

I do myself the Honour of acquainting you that it has pleased God to crown His Majesty's Arms with Success over all His Enemies upon the Ohio, by my having obliged the Enemy to burn and abandon Fort Du Quesne . . . the Enemy . . . being abandoned by their Indians, whom I had previously engaged to leave them.[40]

Forbes certainly deserves credit for insight and patience in supporting the intricate steps leading to the Easton treaty, which had an important effect on changing tribal allegiances. In his efforts against the French and Fort Duquesne, Forbes persisted to the end, in spite of a serious illness that claimed his life shortly after his return to Philadelphia.

The Easton treaty was reinforced by Israel Pemberton and wagon loads of trade goods for the Indians of the Ohio Territory. Just when an era of understanding and tolerance seemed possible, however, the British had decided to refortify the Ohio Forks. Now there would be a permanent British settlement named for William Pitt on the site of the former Fort Duquesne. Both the Quakers and the native tribes were shocked and angered; to the Ohio Indians, this was another indication that the European powers would not leave the Ohio Territory alone. One country or the other would continue to push into Indian land.

Thus ended the dramatically different year of 1758, a year that won the British empire key positions of power. New France had been forced to pull back its frontiers. At enormous expense and effort, William Pitt had succeeded. One hundred years later, in a silent tribute to William Pitt's bold leadership, visitors to the ruins of Louisbourg made the following reflection:

No signs of life [are] visible within these once warlike parapets except the peaceful sheep grazing upon the very brow of the citadel.[41]

Chapter

7 Defeat on the Plains of Abraham

As the year 1759 began, Britain rejoiced and was hopeful. William Pitt had launched a successful New World strategy for England, which was gaining momentum with each victory in North America. Only months after the fall of Louisbourg, Pitt began the next phase of his full campaign against New France.

As a follow-up to Bradstreet's daring seizure of Fort Frontenac, William Johnson and Gen. John Prideaux rebuilt some of the remains of Fort Oswego on Lake Ontario. Their hope was to capture Fort Niagara, between Lakes Ontario and Erie, the critical link in the French chain of forts on the Great Lakes. Meanwhile, General Amherst worked to recover the remnants of the Champlain Valley campaign. It was up to Amherst to succeed where General Abercromby had failed: that is, to work his way past the strongholds of Ticonderoga and Crown Point. Then he

A nineteenth-century illustration of Fort Niagara. The fort, situated on the Niagara River between Lakes Ontario and Erie, was an important French stronghold in the Great Lakes region. The English hoped to break this crucial link in the chain of French forts.

could move down the Champlain Valley to attack Montreal. James Wolfe, commissioned a general after the Louisbourg victory, assembled the naval forces for the expedition up the St. Lawrence River to attack Quebec. New France was being squeezed from all sides.

When the French abandoned and burned Fort Duquesne at the Ohio Forks, the French-leaning members of the Iroquois League moved toward neutrality or even occasional military support of the English. The Senecas reported to William Johnson, superintendent of Indian affairs, that during the winter they had decided to turn against the French. They offered to

Commissioned a general after the Louisbourg victory, James Wolfe headed the naval forces during the assault on Quebec.

help the English capture Fort Niagara, which always had been recognized as a key to French power in the Great Lakes and Ohio region. Without Niagara, the French could not supply their forts farther into the interior.

A party of British regulars and Seneca sailed west from Oswego and arrived at Fort Niagara in early July. Supplied with plenty of artillery, they prepared to bombard the fort. Then an unexpected crisis affected both the British and the French. The Native American warriors in both camps decided not to participate in the battle. Messages and wampum moved back and forth between the Indians, some in the British lines, and some in the French fort. Johnson's Iroquois formed a separate camp from the British, and most of the native people on both sides agreed not to participate in the conflict. This was an example of the complexity of relying on Native American participation in battle situations. Loyalty to tribal principles took priority over actions benefiting Europeans rather than Indians.

The plans of both the French and British commanders were now useless, since each side had far fewer troops than it had counted on. When a French relief column approaching the fort was cut down by the British, however, the commander of Fort Niagara surrendered. By the end of July 1759, Fort Niagara was in British hands.

Victory at Ticonderoga

While Johnson's forces were landing at Niagara, General Amherst led an expedition of about 11,000 British regulars and colo-

Gen. Jeffrey Amherst led British troops to Ticonderoga to conquer the French stronghold.

a by-path in the woods, to the bridge at the sawmills, where finding the bridge standing uninjured, we crossed to the other side. Took possession of a rising ground, drove thence a part of the enemy, killed several. Took a number of prisoners, and routed the whole, before Colonel Haviland's corps had crossed the bridge. The army took possession of the heights near the sawmills, where it lay that night. . . .

July 23: From the time the [British] army came in sight, the enemy kept up a constant fire of cannon from their walls and batteries. The General [Amherst] employed several Provincial [colonial] regiments to transport the cannon and stores across the carrying place; which service they performed with great expedition.[42]

French Troops Retreat

To General Amherst's astonishment, the French troops retreated from the zigzag forward defense line successfully used by Montcalm the year before. Once British cannon shot began falling inside the walls of the fort, the French officer in charge, Bourlemaque, began to plan the evacuation of Ticonderoga. Bourlemaque and most of his troops fled by night in small boats to Crown Point, leaving behind a rear guard to blow up the ammunition they could not carry away. Thousands of British troops watched the fort explode into orange flames. Within days, the fort at nearby Crown Point met the same fate, as the French slipped back toward Canada, leaving burning rubble behind them.

nials on a crucial journey down the Champlain Valley. His goal was to capture the fort at Ticonderoga. In late June, however, he directed the rebuilding of Fort William Henry, postponing his move on Ticonderoga until mid-July.

Rogers' Rangers scouted ahead and discovered the remnants of a bridge crossing the channel between Lakes George and Champlain. General Amherst's engineers repaired the bridge, which the French had failed to completely destroy, thus obtaining quick and easy access to Ticonderoga. British troops then rushed to set up cannon not far from the firing lines of Fort Carillon at Ticonderoga. The advantage of finding the bridge was recorded by Rogers in his journal:

June 22, 1759: The Rangers marched across the mountains, thence through

The Fort at Crown Point

After King George's War ended in 1748, a Swedish naturalist, Peter Kalm, visited the New World and decided to travel from Philadelphia to Canada, through the Champlain Valley. Kalm's careful description of Fort St. Frederic at Crown Point is included in Guy Coolidge's book, The French Occupation of the Champlain Valley from 1609 to 1759.

"July 19 1749. Fort St. Frederic is a fortification on the southern extremity of Lake Champlain, situated on a neck of land, between that Lake and the [Hudson] river. . . . The breadth of this river is here about a good musket-shot. . . . The fort is built on a rock, consisting of black lime-slates . . . ; it is nearly quadrangular, has high and thick walls, made of the same limestone, of which there is a quarry about a half a mile from the fort. On the eastern part of the fort is a high tower [citadel], which is proof against bomb-shells, provided with very thick and substantial walls, and well stored with cannon from the bottom almost to the very top: the governor lives in the tower.

In the terre-plein [raised earthen platform] of the fort is a well-built little church, and houses of stone for the officers and soldiers. There are sharp rocks on all sides towards the land, beyond a cannon shot from the fort. . . . Within one or two musket shots to the east of the fort is a windmill built of stone, with very thick walls, and most of the flour that is wanted to supply the fort is ground here. The Wind-mill is so contrived as to serve the purpose of a redoubt [fortified enclosure], and at the top of it are five or six small pieces of cannon."

Once again, the journal of Robert Rogers provides the chief Ranger's observations of events:

July 23, 1759: At an early hour, the General [Amherst] put his troops in motion. The Rangers were ordered to the front, with directions to proceed across Chesnut plain, the nearest way to Lake Champlain, while two hundred Rangers under Capt. Brewer took possession of a small entrenchment [enemy site] near Lake Champlain, without much loss.

July 24: This day the engineers were employed in raising batteries [cannon placements] with the assistance of a large portion of the troops; Scouts from the Rangers were, during this interval, continually kept out in the vicinity of Crown Point, by whose means the General had hourly intelligence [spy information] from that post. The French, who had previously undermined the Fortress, sprung their mines, which blew up with a tremendous explosion, and immediately commenced a retreat in their boats.[43]

General Amherst halted his huge expedition to spend the remainder of 1759 rebuilding the stone walls and supports of Fort Carillon at Ticonderoga. Fort St. Frederick, the Crown Point stronghold, was only partly destroyed, but the British never completely reconstructed it. Of the two forts, the one at Ticonderoga was located at the more important defensive position.

Amherst also delayed his march toward Montreal to permit his troops to construct a small fleet of ships to patrol Lake Champlain. French warships remained on the lake and would threaten British control of Ticonderoga and Crown Point. This decision left General Wolfe and the British navy in the St. Lawrence River to tackle fortified Quebec alone.

Such changes in plans, however, were typical of British attempts to capture Quebec or Montreal. Failures to carry out a coordinated land and sea attack on New France went as far back as 1690 and the efforts of William Phips. It had been clear for almost seventy years that the capture of Quebec was essential to the defeat of New France.

Attack on the Rock

In spite of General Amherst's delay, Gen. James Wolfe approached his task with enthusiasm. The British expedition left Louisbourg in June 1759 with more than 200 ships and 4,000 troops and arrived near Quebec in three weeks. Wolfe established several encampments along the river opposite the high stony cliffs of the Rock. The city sat on the tip of a peninsula on the north bank, extending into the St. Lawrence River. The St. Charles River flowed along its north and west sides, and

The high bluffs that extend along the north banks of the St. Lawrence River serve as natural fortification for Quebec.

to its east and south were formidable bluffs about 200 feet high. The line of bluffs extended all along the north banks of the St. Lawrence. In this naturally fortified site, the only man-made fortification required was a series of low walls at the top of the Rock, where the city faced inland to the level grassy field known as the Plains of Abraham.

The Marquis de Montcalm was fully prepared for the arrival of the British. He had had time to place about 14,000 troops in and around Quebec and to extend defensive fortifications for six miles east of the Rock along the top of the lower bluffs. West of Quebec were miles of steep cliffs rising directly out of the river, and Montcalm was confident that the great cliffs were adequate protection. French cannon looked down from the city on all the river approaches to Quebec.

For two months, Wolfe waited in the camps along the St. Lawrence for Amherst to arrive from the Champlain Valley. He took the time to think through his plan of attack, exploring several possible landing sites up and down the river. The French followed these movements anxiously. Wolfe, for his part, was aware that if he waited much longer to attack, winter would set in and make a campaign impossible. As the wait stretched into weeks, his troops grew restless, and desertions became common.

The colonial rangers with Wolfe managed a surprise ambush and cleared a French detachment off strategic Pointe Levi, directly across the river from Quebec and its menacing cannon. By setting up artillery on the captured site, the British had put themselves within firing range of the Rock. British troops began to hammer the city with a constant bombardment. The battery on Pointe Levi could not reach the French guns high within the citadel, the fortress on top of the Rock, but the bombing destroyed the lower town, creating hysteria and panic among the largely civilian population.

Wolfe's next move had catastrophic consequences. He directed an attack at

English forces face severe losses as they attempt to reach French troops on the cliffs above.

A British Officer's Journal

Lt. William Henshaw kept a careful record in his "Orderly & Journal" during his stay in 1759 at Fort Edward near the source of the Hudson River. As an officer at the fort, Henshaw had duties ranging from enforcing discipline to care of prisoners. His journal was published in 1909 in Manuscript Records of the French and Indian War *by the American Antiquarian Society.*

"For Edward July 28 1759 Saturday. News by Colo. Amherst that Ticonderoga is in the Hands of the English. The 26th in the Night the French Deserted it after Blowing up one End & Setting it on Fire but the English soon Extinguish'd the Fire; the French made their Escape in Battoes [batteaux]. Information thereof: Rogers Raingers Pursued them, took about Twenty Prisoners & some Plunder.

Sett on a Court Martial to Try two Teamsters for stealing the Kings Flower [flour: a valuable commodity, since food was in short supply]—sent. [Sentence was] 200 [lashes] Each, 1 pardoned the other Recd. 75 Lashes—the Prisoners Pardon't at the News of Ticon. being taken this Afternoon 20 prisoners Came in; the Picquet [picket guard] escorted them. . . .

29 Sunday Report that the Army is getting Battoes into Lake Champlain & preparing to Besiege Crown point—2 or 3 of Connecticut Men came in Wounded.

August 2 Thursday Rainy—This Afternoon Informed that a party of ours went on a scout from Ticonderoga to Crown point They report the French had blown up one Magazene [ammunition storage] set a Fire & Deserted it so they took possession—

August 3 Friday (Fair weather) This Morning at 3 o'clock an Express Ariv'd which gives an Account of Reduction of [Fort] Niagara & 600 of the Enemy made Prisoners—also a French Man the Chief Sagamore of the Indians who always Instigated them to murder & scalp their prisoners."

the eastern end of Montcalm's defensive line, alongside a waterfall that cut into the lower bluffs. The French were well established on the cliffs above the narrow river flats. Their cannon batteries were in place at water level and along the high cliffs.

Under cover of a bombardment from accompanying ships, waves of British troops attempted to scale the cliffs. They were mowed down by the French artillery. Wolfe had hoped to punch a hole in the French line and establish a base on the north side of the river, but the effort was fruitless. More than 400 British and colonial troops were killed or wounded, while the French suffered no casualties.

After this disastrous attempt, Wolfe was desperate. It was September, and winter was closing in. Two letters written to friends of Wolfe and Montcalm, respectively, indicate the separate agonies of the two generals.

Wolfe: The Marquis of Montcalm has a numerous body of armed men (I cannot call it an army), and the strongest country [natural defenses] perhaps in the world. Our fleet blocks up the river above and below the town, but can give no manner of aid in an attack upon the Canadian [French] army. We are now here with about 3600 men, waiting to attack them when and wherever they can best be got at. I am so far recovered as to do business [Wolfe was ill much of the time]; but my constitution is entirely ruined, without the consolation of doing any considerable service to the state, and without any prospect of it.

Montcalm: The night is dark; it rains; our troops are in their tents, with clothes on, ready for an alarm; I in my boots; my horses saddled. In fact, this is my usual way. I wish you were here; for I cannot be everywhere, though I multiply myself, and have not taken off my clothes since the twenty-third of June. . . . I am overwhelmed with work, and should often lose temper, like you do, if I did not remember that I am paid by Europe for not losing it. Nothing new since my last [letter]. I give the enemy another month, or less, to stay here.[44]

Wolfe decided he must risk a new approach to the city. He directed his ships to make their way, one by one, past the citadel's guns under cover from the British cannon on Pointe Levi. A scout had recognized a narrow footpath up the steep cliffs north of the city, guarded by only a few French pickets. Wolfe managed to draw away Montcalm's troop strength and divert his attention by sending a decoy force to another landing site. Then Wolfe began a daring plan to reach the level ground at the top of the cliffs.

About 1,700 British troops landed in the dark at the narrow river's edge, soon to be known as Wolfe's Cove. General Wolfe was in the first landing party. The first scouts to reach the crest of the cliffs surprised the dozing pickets and opened the way for the surging file of British troops to rush to the top. By the time dawn warmed

Hoping to catch Montcalm off guard, Wolfe, forging his way to the river's edge, leads his troops on a daring attack at Quebec.

Suffering from a fatal bullet through his lungs, Wolfe is carried off the battlefield. The British victory at the Battle of Quebec put a virtual end to the French and Indian War.

the sky on September 13, more than 400 British troops were ready in formation, led by James Wolfe in the front rank. The rows of redcoats became visible as daylight appeared on the Plains of Abraham.

Wolfe and Montcalm

At this last great standoff between the British and French empires in the New World, the two assembled armies pre-

pared for battle in the classic European tradition. Montcalm, caught off guard, gathered as many troops as possible on the Plains of Abraham and organized them into formation. The two armies were similar in size, and they now prepared to exhibit their rigorous and formal European training. Advancing toward each other in precise lines to drumrolls and bagpipes, the ranks opened fire at forty yards, reloaded, and advanced. A British bayonet charge followed the initial musket fire, scattering the French ranks, which

In this early illustration, Montcalm lies dying after France's defeat on the Plains of Abraham.

then fled in retreat. James Wolfe fell, a bullet through his lungs, and the Marquis de Montcalm lay dying, hit by an artillery shell. Neither commander survived the great battle on the Plains of Abraham. A senior French officer wrote home: "No rout was ever more complete than that of our army. Posterity will hardly believe it."[45]

The city of Quebec surrendered on September 18, and the most decisive battle of the French and Indian War was over. One of the great events of world history, the British victory on the Plains of Abraham settled forever the struggle between England and France for control over North America.

8 Under One Flag

The French and Indian War dragged on for another year after the surrender of Quebec, but New France was the clear loser. In the summer of 1760, General Amherst's troops resumed their progress down the Champlain Valley and the Richelieu River. The expedition now targeted Montreal. Unlike the Rock of Quebec, Montreal had few natural defenses. Using eighteenth-century maps in the British Museum in London, historian Francis Parkman described the old city as follows:

> The Montreal of that time was a long, narrow assemblage of wooden or stone houses, one or two stories high, above which rose the peaked towers of the

Seminary, the spires of three churches, the walls of four convents, with the trees of their adjacent gardens, and, conspicuous at the lower end, a high mound of earth, crowned by a redoubt, where a few cannon were mounted. The whole was surrounded by a shallow moat and a stone wall, made for defence against Indians, and incapable of resisting cannon.[46]

Joining Amherst at Montreal were William Johnson's troops from Fort Niagara and a contingent of Wolfe's troops from Quebec. Finally, a well-coordinated conjunction of British forces met at the St. Lawrence to confront Montreal. With the

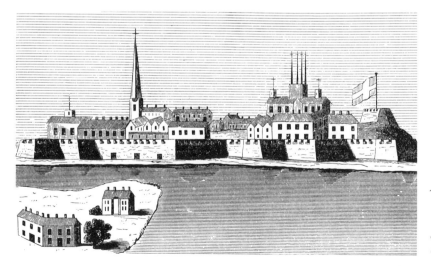

A depiction of Montreal in 1760, the year that Governor Vaudreuil surrendered the city, along with the rest of Canada, to the British crown.

Rogers Takes Fort Detroit

Immediately after the fall of Quebec to the British in 1759, Robert Rogers was dispatched to take the French forts in the western territory. His last communication to the French commander at Detroit, followed by his description of securing the fort as British territory, appears in Reminiscences of the French War.

"Sir:

I acknowledge the receipt of your two letters yesterday. . . . The enclosed letter from the Marquis de Vaudreuil will inform you of the surrender of Canada; of the indulgence granted to the inhabitants; and the terms allowed to the troops of His Most Christian Majesty [Louis XV, the king of France]. Capt. Campbell will shew you the capitulation [document of surrender]. I beg you will not detain him, as I have Gen. Amherst's orders immediately to relieve the place [seize the fort]. My troops will halt without [outside] the town till four o'clock, when I shall expect your answer.

The inhabitants of Detroit shall not be molested, they and you complying with the capitulation. They shall be protected in their estates and shall not be pillaged [robbed] by my Indians, nor yours who have joined me.

Yours, &c   R. Rogers"

French troops deserting him and his town desperate for provisions, Governor Vaudreuil surrendered Montreal and all of Canada to the British crown in September 1760.

Joyous celebrations swept through the British colonies, particularly New England. The governor of Massachusetts proclaimed a day of thanksgiving, and Bostonians celebrated with a parade, a grand dinner in Faneuil Hall, music, bonfires, the firing of cannon, and sermons celebrating the end of the war. From the pulpit of the "Old Church in Boston" came the following words:

Long had it been the common opinion, Canada must be conquered, or we could hope for no lasting quiet in these parts; and now through the good hand of our God upon us, we see the happy day of its accomplishment. We behold His Majesty's victorious troops treading upon the high places of the enemy, their last fortress delivered up, and their whole country surrendered to the King of Britain in the person of his General, the intrepid, the serene, the successful Amherst.[47]

The French forts in the continent's interior, which were many miles apart, had survived for years on their own, too distant for support from the government in Quebec. Thus in the Ohio country, quick, decisive skirmishes to establish British control continued for several years. Later in 1760, after the fall of Montreal, Robert Rogers and his Rangers moved swiftly to take Fort Detroit from the French. Gradually the remaining frontier forts exchanged their French flags of fleur-de-lis for the British Union Jack.

Changing Times

As soon as the French threat had been removed, the population pressure from the English seaboard colonies pushed immediately over the Appalachian Mountains into the frontier territory. For the tribes beyond the mountains, the flood of settlers threatened to end the tradi-tional Indian way of life. Treaties and land agreements made during the French and Indian War were disregarded, or misinterpreted to the advantage of the colonists. Feeling betrayed by the English, Native Americans fought back. It would be difficult to prevent wars with the native tribes for control of western lands, and William Johnson stated the situation well: "The Six Nations, Western Indians, etc., having never been conquered, either by the English or French, nor subject to their Laws, consider themselves a free people."[48]

Pontiac's War, begun in 1763 and ending in 1765, was a warning of troubles to come. Pontiac, an Ottawa leader in Michigan territory, was greatly influenced by the teaching of Neolin, "the Prophet." Neolin

Ottawa leader Pontiac holds a council with his tribe. When British colonists threatened Indian territory, Pontiac led an uprising against them.

taught that the future strength of the Indians lay in resisting the Europeans and Christianity and returning to traditional Indian ways. After decades of interaction with French, English, and Spanish cultures, Pontiac's followers led a crusade to turn away the European tide.

Once Detroit had fallen to the British, many tribes in the "Northwest" territory of Michigan, Ohio, Indiana, and Illinois rebelled against British authority. Under the French, there had been few settlers and no restraints on hunting lands. The relationship between the French traders and Indian cultures was generally cooperative. The English, however, claimed and settled the land with permanent farms and towns, forcing the native people into smaller and smaller spaces. For the Indians, it was easy to see that their ability to survive was threatened.

As more and more Indian people joined Pontiac in his resistance to English expansion, Pontiac said, "It is important, my brothers, that we exterminate from our lands this nation which seeks only to destroy us."[49] Pontiac's War spread quickly throughout the west, with only the forts at Detroit, Niagara, and Pittsburgh holding out; all the smaller and more remote garrisons fell to the Indians. The frontier forts consisted of a few basic log buildings surrounded by sturdy high fence walls. At least one corner of the wall supported a lookout tower. In recording Pontiac's first encounter with the commander of Fort Detroit, author Alvin Josephy Jr. gives a good account of fort design at a strategic western fortress:

Unaware that the British officer knew of his plans, Pontiac confidently led his people across the river on the morning

Pontiac's invaders launch a night attack on a European schooner protecting Fort Detroit.

of May 7, 1763, and approached the east gate of the post. The fort was the largest and strongest in the west, with a wall of cedar pickets about fifteen feet high and twelve hundred yards in circumference, enclosing what amounted to a small village. Guarded by bastions at three of its corners and by two small, detached blockhouses, the post stood on a slope that ran down to the river, with one of its walls and gates fronting on the water. Inside the fort Gladwin [the fort commander] had two six-pound cannons, one three-pounder, and three mortars, as well as a force of approximately one hundred and twenty soldiers and perhaps thirty or forty English traders who could assist in the defense. In the river, also protecting the post, were a two-masted schooner, the *Huron*, of six guns, and a larger sloop, the *Michigan*.[50]

The British government announced the Proclamation Act of 1763 partly in response to Pontiac's War. The original idea began with the Easton treaty of 1758, which had created boundaries guaranteeing certain lands for Indian use. The treaty was useful during the French and Indian War, since it was instrumental in keeping the Ohio Territory Indians from aiding the French. After the war, however, the English colonies were more concerned about preventing war between English settlers and the Indian tribes. The act of 1763 prohibited English settlers from moving into lands across the Appalachian Mountains that were designated Indian territory. The proclamation stated:

It is just and reasonable, and essential to our Interest and the Security of our Colonies, that the several Nations or tribes of Indians with whom We are connected, and who live under our

Victory Celebrations

All over New England, celebrations of victory in God's name were delivered from Puritan pulpits. These remarks, by Eli Forbes, who had served as chaplain to a Massachusetts regiment, are in Montcalm and Wolfe *by Francis Parkman. Forbes's sermon to his small congregation reflects the New England perspective on the military and on divine providence.*

"God has given us to sing this day the downfall of New France, the North American Babylon, New England's rival. . . . Thus God was our salvation and our strength; yet he who directs the great events of war suffered not our joy to be uninterrupted. For we had to lament the fall of the valiant and good General Wolfe, whose death demands a tear from every British eye, a sigh from every Protestant heart. Is he dead? I recall myself. Such heroes are immortal; he lives on every loyal tongue; he lives in every grateful breast; and charity bids me give him a place among the princes of heaven. . . .

What fair hopes arise from the peaceful and undisturbed enjoyment of this good land, and the blessing of our gracious God with it! Methinks I see towns enlarged, settlements increased, and this howling wilderness become a fruitful field which the Lord hath blessed; and, to complete the scene, I see churches rise and flourish in every Christian grace where has been the seat of Satan and Indian idolatry."

Protection, should not be molested or disturbed in the Possession of such Parts of our Dominions and Territories. Not having been ceded to or purchased by Us, [they] are reserved to them, as their Hunting Grounds.[51]

No one found the Proclamation Act satisfactory, however. Boundaries drawn in London existed only on paper, and both tribal people and colonists crossed them. While the Indians welcomed the proclamation, they did not feel any connection to the artificial lines established by the colonies. No one was sent to the vast frontier territory to enforce the rules, and every colony submitted requests to London for exceptions to be made in one land transaction after another.

The final change in colonial control of North America and the heritage of long contact with Europeans spelled the beginning of the end of traditional Native American life. After 1760, native people lost their leverage in tilting the balance of power back and forth between colonial

Pontiac's peace offering to Major Rogers ended Pontiac's War.

George Croghan was the most experienced English trader with the Native Americans in the Ohio Valley. He predicted problems between the British and the tribes. His observations are recorded in Red, White and Black *by Gary Nash.*

"[The Indians] had great expectations of being very generally supplied by us, and from their poverty and mercenary [military] disposition they can't bear such a disappointment. Undoubtedly the general [Amherst] has his own reason for not allowing any present or ammunition to be given them, and I wish [this policy] may have its desired effect. But I take this opportunity to acquaint you that I dread the event as I know Indians can't long persevere. . . . Their success at the beginning of this war on our frontiers is too recent in their memory for them to consider their present inability to make war with us. And if the Senecas, Delawares, and Shawnees should break with us, it will end in a general war with all western nations."

empires. Once England had gained control, the Indian nations became less and less independent and influential. The Native American way of life on the North American continent was forever altered.

Treaty Negotiations

No official treaty could be signed to end the French and Indian War until the conflict in Europe—the Seven Years' War—had ended. In fact, for several years after the fall of Canada in 1760, the war continued to expand in Europe and around the world. Two years later, the British navy had circled the globe and raised the Union Jack in distant ports in the name of the empire. George III, who became king in 1762 after the death of his grandfather

George II, dismissed William Pitt for overextending the empire at the expense of the treasury. The new king decided it was time to end the Seven Years' War, now that victory in North America had been achieved. The French military effort in Europe had finally collapsed, and treaties had been negotiated between France and Russia, Sweden, Austria, and Germany.

France was also ready to consider a treaty with England, her long-time enemy. Like their British counterparts, the French were also broke. France had been devastated by the French and Indian War, in which it lost its reputation as a nation able to stand and fight heroically. It also lost all but a small fragment of the entire New World in which the country had invested for almost 250 years.

According to the terms of the Peace of Paris, signed in 1763, Great Britain as victor, claimed all the territories of present-day Canada. This included the region of Acadia and all the territory east of the Mississippi previously controlled by France. Much of Florida was transferred from Spain to England, since Spain had joined the losing side, allying itself with France to fight against England. The North American continent was now divided in half by the Mississippi River. The British held all the land to the east except for the city of New Orleans, which the French retained. Control of the rest of the continent was in the hands of the French and Spanish.

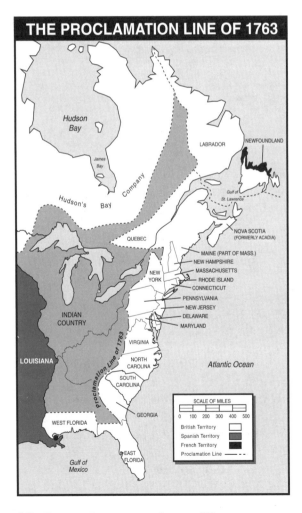

THE PROCLAMATION LINE OF 1763

Hudson Bay

James Bay

Hudson's Bay Company

LABRADOR

NEWFOUNDLAND

Gulf of St. Lawrence

NOVA SCOTIA (FORMERLY ACADIA)

QUEBEC

MAINE (PART OF MASS.)
NEW HAMPSHIRE
MASSACHUSETTS
RHODE ISLAND
CONNECTICUT
PENNSYLVANIA
NEW JERSEY
DELAWARE
MARYLAND

NEW YORK

INDIAN COUNTRY

Proclamation Line of 1763

VIRGINIA

NORTH CAROLINA

SOUTH CAROLINA

Atlantic Ocean

LOUISIANA

GEORGIA

WEST FLORIDA

EAST FLORIDA

Gulf of Mexico

SCALE OF MILES
0 100 200 300 400 500

British Territory
Spanish Territory
French Territory
Proclamation Line - - -

Rule Britannia

The British now ruled the seas, controlled a third of North America, and appeared to be supremely powerful. However, the empire was spread thinly throughout the world and burdened with debt from decades of European and American wars. The ten years after the end of the French and Indian War in 1763 witnessed a series of events that would lead into the next significant war in North America, the War of Independence.

First, the British colonists greatly resented the Proclamation Act of 1763. They had waited all through the French and Indian War for the western territory to be safe for expansion. Now they were told they would not be allowed to move across the mountains. Next, a series of new taxes was placed on the colonies to pay England's war debts and to support the large British army that remained in North America. Throughout the French and Indian War, the English colonists had sacrificed time, money, and even their lives. Not only did they resent being burdened with extra taxes after the war had been won, but they saw no need for the British troops to remain in North America.

The English colonies resented the British Crown's control and objected to the restrictions placed on them. Having seen the pettiness and ineptitude of many British political and military leaders during the French and Indian War, they no longer believed the empire to be invincible. The English colonists had also gained confidence in their political, military, and economic skills. They viewed their own leaders as equal in strength, persistence, and intelligence to any in Europe. They

The French and Indian War paved the way for the split between the colonists and the British crown. A prelude to the American Revolution, colonists tar and feather a tax collector to vividly demonstrate their resentment of British taxes.

were proud of their role in the French and Indian War.

The groundwork for an independent nation had been laid. As one historian put it, "Wars have a way, when they end, of be-ing only a beginning."[52] Thirteen years after the end of the French and Indian War, the English colonies in North America declared war on Great Britain. The American Revolution had begun.

Notes

Chapter 1: Old Enemies Meet in a New World

1. John Smith, "A Description of New England [1616]." Quoted in Paul Lauter, gen. ed., *The Heath Anthology of American Literature*. Lexington, MA: Heath, 1990.
2. John Winthrop, "A Modell of Christian Charity [1630]." Quoted in *Heath Anthology*.
3. Quoted in Allyn B. Forbes, ed., *Winthrop Papers*, vol. 2. Boston: Massachusetts Historical Society, 1929-1947.
4. Samuel de Champlain, "The Voyages to the Great River St. Lawrence [1608-1612]." Quoted in *Heath Anthology*.

Chapter 2: Spreading Flames

5. Daniel Sanders, *A History of the Indian Wars with the First Settlers of the United States, Particularly in New England*. Montpelier, VT: Wright & Sibley, 1812.
6. Sanders, *History of the Indian Wars*.
7. Samuel Adams Drake, *The Border Wars of New England*. Williamstown, MA: Corner House Publishers, 1897. Reprinted 1973.
8. John Williams, *The Redeemed Captive, Returning to Zion*. E. Clark, ed., Amherst: University of Massachusetts Press, 1976.
9. Drake, *Border Wars of New England*.
10. Drake, *Border Wars of New England*.

Chapter 3: A Mighty Fortress

11. Samuel Adams Drake, *The Taking of Louisbourg, 1745*. Boston: Lee & Shepardy, 1890.
12. Quoted in Blaine Adams, "The Construction and Occupation of the Barracks of the King's Bastion at Louisbourg," *Canadian Historic Sites, 18*, Occasional Papers in Archaeology and History. Ottawa: National Historic Parks and Sites Branch Parks Canada, 1978.
13. Quoted in Raymond F. Baker, "A Campaign of Amateurs: The Siege of Louisbourg, 1745," *Canadian Historic Sites, 18*.
14. Quoted in Baker, "A Campaign of Amateurs."
15. Journal of Stephen Williams. Quoted by Louis Effingham DeForest, in *Louisbourg Journals, 1745*. New York: Society of Colonial Wars in the State of New York, 1932.
16. Baker, "A Campaign of Amateurs."

Chapter 4: Sparks in the Wilderness

17. Quoted in Samuel Eliot Morison, *The Oxford History of the American People*. New York: Oxford University Press, 1965.
18. Quoted in Francis Jennings, *Empire of Fortune: Crowns, Colonies & Tribes in the Seven Years' War in America*. New York: Norton, 1988.
19. Quoted in Jennings, *Empire of Fortune*.
20. Quoted in Jennings, *Empire of Fortune*.
21. Quoted in Jennings, *Empire of Fortune*.
22. Quoted in Francis Russell, *The French and Indian Wars*. New York: American Heritage, 1962.
23. Quoted in Russell, *The French and Indian Wars*.
24. Quoted in Russell, *The French and Indian Wars*.
25. Quoted in Russell, *The French and Indian Wars*.

Chapter 5: The Champlain Valley Crucible: 1755-1756

26. Quoted in Jennings, *Empire of Fortune*.
27. Quoted in Jennings, *Empire of Fortune*.

28.   Quoted in *Reminiscences of the French War, Containing Rogers's Expeditions, the Life and Memoirs of John Stark*. Freedom, NH: Freedom Historical Society, 1988.

29.   Quoted in Edward P. Hamilton, *The French and Indian Wars*. Garden City, NY: Doubleday, 1962.

30.   Quoted in Hamilton, *The French and Indian Wars*.

31.   Quoted in Morison, *The Oxford History of the American People*.

Chapter 6: Master Plan for Victory

32.   Quoted in Jennings, *Empire of Fortune*.

33.   Quoted in Baker, "A Campaign of Amateurs."

34.   Quoted in *Reminiscences from the French War (Rogers's Expeditions)*.

35.   Harrison Bird, *Battle for a Continent: The French and Indian War, 1754-1763*. New York: Oxford University Press, 1965.

36.   Quoted in Jennings, *Empire of Fortune*.

37.   Quoted in Jennings, *Empire of Fortune*.

38.   Quoted in Jennings, *Empire of Fortune*.

39.   Quoted in Jennings, *Empire of Fortune*.

40.   Quoted in Jennings, *Empire of Fortune*.

41.   Quoted in Adams, "The Construction and Occupation of Louisbourg."

Chapter 7: Defeat on the Plains of Abraham

42.   Quoted in *Reminiscences of the French War (Rogers's Expeditions)*.

43.   Quoted in *Reminiscences of the French War (Rogers's Expeditions)*.

44.   Quoted in Francis Parkman, *Montcalm and Wolfe*, Vol. III. Boston: Little, Brown, 1902.

45.   Quoted in Hamilton, *The French and Indian Wars*.

Chapter 8: Under One Flag

46.   Parkman, *Montcalm and Wolfe*.

47.   Quoted in Parkman, *Montcalm and Wolfe*.

48.   Quoted in Gary B. Nash, *Red, White and Black: The Peoples of Early America*. Englewood Cliffs, NJ: Prentice-Hall, 1982.

49.   Quoted in Nash, *Red, White and Black*.

50.   Alvin M. Josephy Jr., *The Patriot Chiefs: A Chronicle of American Indian Resistance*. New York: Penguin Books, 1976.

51.   Quoted in Nash, *Red, White and Black*.

52.   Russell, *The French and Indian Wars*.

Glossary

Acadia: an area colonized by the French that included Nova Scotia, Cape Breton Island, and parts of present-day Maine

aide-de-camp: an assistant to a military officer

alliance: a mutual assistance agreement between two or more nations or groups

anarchy: a state of confusion, disorder, and chaos, usually meaning no government in operation

balance of power: evenness of strength, preventing any one nation from becoming strong enough to dominate or interfere with another

bastion: a strengthened section of a fort

broadside: the long side of a ship

buffer colony: a colony created to protect a country's other colonies, to absorb attacks, or to provide extra space between the other original colonies and hostile groups

cold war: intense hostility and rivalry between two nations, sustained without the use of violence

confederacy: an alliance uniting two or more area governments for mutual benefit

converts: persons who have been persuaded to adopt new ideas, usually religious ideas

etiquette: manners; the proper way of doing something

flotilla: a small unit of naval vessels

formidable: difficult to overcome; impressive

garrison: (noun) a body of troops stationed at a fort; (verb) to supply a fort with troops

immigrant: a person who has moved to one country from another

implacable: unbending

Iroquois: a strong union of Native American tribes: the Oneida, Cayuga, Onondaga, Mohawk, and Seneca; later joined by a sixth tribe, the Tuscarora

Jesuit: a Roman Catholic priest of the order, the Society of Jesus

loon: a freshwater bird common in northern regions of North America

maize: corn

marquis: a nobleman ranking below a duke and above an earl or count

monopolize: dominate

mortar: a fat, wide-mouthed cannon capable of firing at high angles (for example, over the wall of a fort)

patent: a document verifying ownership

peremptory: decisive, final

picket: (noun) stout pointed posts used in walls to protect settlements; (verb) to guard or be on watch

portage: (noun) the land connecting two bodies of water; (verb) to carry cargo overland from one body of water to another

posterity: all future generations; descendants

prohibit: to prevent from occurring

Quakers: a religious group that is opposed to war and violence

ragtag: riffraff; disorderly and unpresentable

ransom: payment made for the freeing of a captive or prisoner

redoubt: a fortification separate from the fort, usually placed to defend a certain site

rout: a major defeat in which an army turns and flees rather than making an orderly retreat

slovenly: dirty and uncared for

squadron: a portion of a fleet of ships

stockade: a high protective fence

succession: the order in which one monarch was replaced by another

undeclared war: a period of battles between two nations in the absence of a formal declaration of war

watershed: highest point from which water flows in one direction, such as the highest mountain point or ridge

For Further Reading

Nancy Bonvillain, *The Mohawk.* New York: Chelsea House, 1992. Colin G. Calloway, *The Abenaki.* New York: Chelsea House, 1989. Barbara Graymont, *The Iroquois.* New York: Chelsea House, 1988. These three volumes belong to the excellent Indians of North America Series: well-written, well-illustrated books for young people that offer accurate historic and contemporary information about Native American people.

Lincoln Dexter, *Maps of Early Massachusetts.* Rev. ed. Sturbridge, MA: Lincoln Dexter, 1984. Dexter's book is very interesting for young people since it includes summaries of New England coastal explorations, geological and archaeological background related to Native American settlement in the region, and a fascinating series of maps from 1606 to 1700. Bibliographies, charts of Indian place names, deeds, and records of court disputes supplement the text. Available in paperback.

Virginia Hamilton, *In the Beginning: Creation Stories from Around the World.* New York: Harcourt Brace Jovanovich, 1988. This engaging Newberry Award-winning book provides an important cross section of very readable creation stories, including several from North American cultures. Available in paperback.

Francis Parkman, *Montcalm and Wolfe.* [France and England in North America, Part Seventh], Vol. III. Boston: Little, Brown, 1902. Reprint editions available. There are many more recent books about the French and Indian War but Parkman's telling of the story, primarily from the British viewpoint, is still a good one. Newer material about the role of Native Americans should be sought to balance Parkman's nineteenth-century biases, however.

Reminiscences of the French War. Containing Rogers's Expeditions, the Life and Memoirs of John Stark. Freedom, NH: Freedom Historical Society, 1988. Shortly after the end of the French and Indian War, Robert Rogers of Rogers' Rangers recorded his memoirs of the war, which were printed in Boston in 1765. This is a paperback reprint of the 1831 edition, which included Stark's writings. It is a very dramatic narrative of events primarily in the Champlain Valley. Excellent for young readers because the language has been modernized and made uniform.

Francis Russell, *The French and Indian Wars.* New York: American Heritage, 1962. Part of the Junior Library series, this volume is an ideal introduction for young people to the series of wars in the New World from 1690 to 1763 between the French and English. Very readable with excellent illustrations, the book uses many story vignettes to illustrate the times; unfortunately, its view of Native Americans is very dated and biased, and other books should be consulted for balance.

Mary P. Wells Smith, *The Boy Captive of Old Deerfield*. Deerfield, MA: Pocumtuck Valley Memorial Association, 1979. First published in 1904, 200 years after the events described, this was the first of the Old Deerfield series of four historical novels. Through the eyes of ten-year-old Stephen Williams, it tells the story of the attack on Deerfield, Massachusetts, in 1704 by the French and Abenaki and Stephen's captivity in Canada. In *Boy Captive in Canada*, part two of the story, Stephen finally returns home. Stephen's father, Rev. John Williams, wrote his own captivity account, *The Redeemed Captive, Returning to Zion*, published in 1707.

Henry Woodhead, ed., *Realm of the Iroquois*. Alexandria, VA: Time-Life Books, 1993. One of six volumes in the series The American Indians, this book is beautifully illustrated, including important maps, diagrams, and historic photographs. Perhaps most important is the specific inclusion of material about modern Iroquois, their lives, and recent history. While the text may be challenging for some, the book is primarily visual and therefore bound to be appealing to young people.

Additional Works Consulted

Raymond F. Baker, "A Campaign of Amateurs: The Siege of Louisbourg, 1745," *Canadian Historic Sites No. 18*. Quebec: Ministry of Supply and Services Canada, 1978. This excellent and readable study is based on research at the Fortress of Louisbourg archive at the historic site. It is accompanied by interesting maps and photographs.

Harrison Bird, *Battle for a Continent: The French and Indian War, 1754-1763*. New York: Oxford University Press, 1965. Bird is a military historian, and his accounts of the campaigns are detailed and well written.

Guy Omeron Coolidge, *The French Occupation of the Champlain Valley from 1609 to 1759*. Harrison, NY: Harbor Hill Books, 1979. Originally published in 1938 by the Vermont Historical Society, this book is well documented, and includes interesting primary material. Its primary focus is on Fort St. Frederic at Crown Point.

Edward P. Hamilton, *The French and Indian Wars*. Garden City, NY: Doubleday, 1962. Hamilton was director of the Fort Ticonderoga historic site when he wrote this account of the forts and battles of the wars between the French and English between 1689 and 1763, as well as general background information for the Mainstream of America Series.

Francis Jennings, *Empire of Fortune: Crowns, Colonies & Tribes in the Seven Years' War in America*. New York: Norton, 1988. Jennings's book emphasizes the relationships between Native Americans and the French and English, attempting to view the French and Indian War through non-European eyes. This book has excellent Native American source material.

Alvin M. Josephy Jr., *The Patriot Chiefs*. New York: Penguin Books, 1976. Readable and fairly thorough, this book focuses on several of the great historic Native American leaders, including Pontiac, who was prominent in the period between the French and Indian War and the American Revolution.

Edward Larrabee, "Archaeological Research at the Fortress of Louisbourg, 1961-1965," *Canadian Historic Sites No. 2*. Ontario: National Historic Sites Service, 1971. This interesting academic study is supplemented with excellent photographs and maps.

Paul Lauter, ed., *The Heath Anthology of American Literature*, Vol. I. Lexington, MA: Heath, 1990. This anthology contains more than 400 pages of primary material from the history of North America before the American Revolution.

Samuel Eliot Morison, *The Oxford History of the American People*. New York: Oxford University Press, 1965. Morison writes passionately and inclusively about American history. This distinguished historian's ability to emphasize themes and connections is extremely valuable. Besides, Morison is great fun to read and always memorable.

Gary B. Nash, *Red, White and Black: The Peoples of Early America*. Englewood

Cliffs, NJ: Prentice-Hall, 1982. Nash writes of interactions between three major cultures—European, Native American, and African—and describes how each adapted to and interacted with the others in colonial times. Engaging and well organized, the book gives excellent background information on non-European cultures that is usually overlooked.

John Williams, *The Redeemed Captive, Returning to Zion*. E. Clark, ed., Amherst: University of Massachusetts Press, 1976. This publication of the original 1707 edition, with background introduction and notes for the text, is a good example of the "captivity" literature that was widely read during the first half of the eighteenth century. Six editions of this account were published between 1707 and 1795. It tells the story of the French and Abenaki attack on the village outpost of Deerfield, Massachusetts, in 1704, the forced march to Canada of the 111 captives, and the encounters of these colonial Protestants with Native American life and French Roman Catholic culture.

Research Bibliography

These interesting accounts for research are available at the Memorial Libraries, Deerfield, Massachusetts, which house the special collection of the Pocumtuck Valley Memorial Association.

Louis Effingham DeForest, *Louisbourg Journals, 1745.* New York: Society of Colonial Wars in the State of New York, 1932. This valuable publication of ten journals, with seven appendices, includes the journals of Stephen Williams and John Bradstreet. Six of the journals are anonymous.

Samuel Adams Drake, *The Border Wars of New England.* Williamstown, MA: Corner House Publishers, 1973. Reprint of 1897 edition. *The Taking of Louisbourg, 1745.* Boston: Lee & Shepard, 1890. Drake's writings are enjoyable, early historical overviews of the period of the French and Indian War (from the mid-1600s to 1763). Some volumes have been reprinted.

Luke Gridley's Diary of 1757. Hartford, CT: Hartford Press, The Case, Lockwood & Brainard Co., 1906. Edited for the Acorn Club, a private book club. A captain from Farmington, Connecticut, Gridley was based at Fort Edward at the Carrying Place between the Hudson River and Lake George. His diary, printed in the writer's colloquial English, provides good examples of daily tasks, illnesses, and administra-tion of discipline in a frontier fort. It is introduced by a lively preface.

Manuscript Records of the French and Indian War. Worcester, MA: American Antiquarian Society, 1909. A listing of the letters and documents by William Johnson and John Bradstreet, and William Henshaw's Orderly Book, with a brief summary about each such document in the society's possession. A few complete manuscripts, such as George Washington's letter to Governor Dinwiddie after Braddock's defeat, are included.

Narrative of Titus King of Northampton, Massachusetts. Hartford, CT: Connecticut Historical Society, 1938. Reprinted fascimile. King, who was captured outside Rice's Fort at Charlemont, Massachusetts, in 1755, relates in a very personal, unaffected style his experiences with his Indian captors and French Catholic priests.

Daniel Sanders, *A History of the Indian Wars with the First Settlers of the U.S., Particularly in New England.* Montpelier, VT: Wright & Sibley, 1812. Although somewhat difficult to read because of its small size and early typeface, this volume offers interesting perspectives from the early 1800s on the French and Indian raids of the seventeenth century.

Index

Picture Credits

Cover photo: North Wind Picture Archives

Library of Congress, 10, 15 (both), 17 (both), 18, 19, 20, 21, 22, 23 (bottom), 27, 28, 37, 39, 45, 46 (both), 47, 48 (both), 49, 50, 51, 52, 56, 57, 58 (left), 60 (both), 62, 64 (bottom), 68, 70, 71, 74, 76, 79, 80, 81, 83, 87, 88, 94, 97

North Wind Picture Archives, 12, 13, 25, 30, 53, 64 (top)

Stock Montage, Inc., 14, 23 (top), 29, 32, 41, 43, 54, 58 (right), 66, 84, 86, 89, 91, 92

About the Authors

Benton Minks has a master's degree in American literature and teaches English at Amherst Regional High School in Amherst, Massachusetts. He has written *One Hundred Best Hitters* about baseball and is coauthor of *Baseball Managers*.

Louise Minks has a master's degree in American history and has written *The Hudson River School*, a book about America's first landscape painters. She is also an artist, a teacher, and a member of the education staff of Memorial Hall Museum in Deerfield, Massachusetts. A lover of art and books, Louise has written and illustrated two limited-edition handmade books.

Benton and Louise Minks have lived in Leverett, Massachusetts, for twenty years, with their daughters, Leah and Erin. They are active in town government and regional historical activities. This is the second book for young people that they have written together. The first was *The Revolutionary War*.